Economic Revolutions in Britain 1750–1850

Prometheus unbound?

Richard Brown

Manshead School
Dunstable

The right of the
University of Cambridge
to print and sell
all manner of books
was granted by
Henry VIII in 1534.
The University has printed
and published continuously
since 1584.

CAMBRIDGE UNIVERSITY PRESS

Cambridge
New York   Port Chester
Melbourne   Sydney

Published by the Press Syndicate of the University of Cambridge
The Pitt Building, Trumpington Street, Cambridge CB2 1RP
40 West 20th Street, New York, NY 10011-4211, USA
10 Stamford Road, Oakleigh, Victoria 3166, Australia

First published 1992

Printed in Great Britain at the University Press, Cambridge

British Library cataloguing in publication data
Brown, Richard
    Economic revolutions 1750–1850: Prometheus unbound?
    1. Economic development, history
    I. Title
    330.9

ISBN 0 521 39785 5

Cover illustration *The Iron Forge between Dolgelli and Barmouth, Merionethshire*, by Paul Sandby. Published in *Welsh Views*, 1776.

Notice to teachers

VN

020469

Contents

iii

For Margaret, for understanding and time

Acknowledgements

The author and publisher would like to thank the following for permission to reproduce extracts and illustrations:

Extracts 1.10, 1.11, 1.12 E.A. Wrigley and R.S. Schofield, *The Population History of England 1541–1871: A Reconstitution*, 1989; 1.10, 5.6 P. Deane and W.A. Cole, *British Economic Growth, 1688 1969*, 1969; 5.2, 5.7 B.R. Mitchell and P. Deane, *Abstract of British Historical Statistics*, 1962; 5.5 P. Deane, *The First Industrial Revolution*, 1965; 6.10c E.A. Wrigley (ed.), *Nineteenth Century Society*, 1972; all reproduced by permission of Cambridge University Press. 1.11 N. Tranter, *Population since the Industrial Revolution*, Croom Helm, 1973; 5.3, 5.4 R. Davis, 'English foreign trade 1700–1774', in W.E. Minchinton (ed.), *The Growth of Overseas Trade in the 17th and 18th Centuries*, Methuen, 1969; 1.20 P. O'Farrell, *England and Ireland since 1800*, 1975; 5.2 E.B. Schumpeter, *English Overseas Trade Statistics 1697–1808*, 1960; 5.8 W. Schlote, *British Overseas Trade from 1700 to the 1930s*, 1952; 5.9 A.H. Imlah, *Economic Elements in the Pax Britannica*, 1958; 6.10(a–e) A. Howe, *The Cotton Masters 1830–1860*, 1984; 6.11 R.E. Cameron (ed.), *Banking in the Early Stages of Industrialisation*, 1967; all reproduced by permission of the Oxford University Press; 3.16 A.E. Musson, *The Growth of British Industry*, Batsford, 1978; 4.18 C. Harvie, *The Industrialisation Process 1830–1914*, The Open University, 1971; 5.6 E. Pawson, *The Early Industrial Revolution*, Batsford, 1978; 5.10c Voltaire, *Letters on England*, translated by Leonard Tancock, Penguin, 1980, copyright © Leonard Tancock 1980, reproduced by permission of Penguin Books Ltd; 5.13 Sophie von La Roche, *Sophie in London 1786*, translated by Clare Williams, Jonathan Cape Ltd, reproduced by permission of Penguin Books Ltd; 6.1 R.H. Tawney, *Religion and the Rise of Capitalism*, John Murray, 1926.

Illustrations 2.18 The Trustees, The National Gallery, London; 2.19 Ashmolean Museum, Oxford; 2.20 The Mansell Collection; 2.21 Manchester City Art Galleries ©.

Every effort has been made to reach copyright holders; the publishers would be glad to hear from anyone whose rights they have unknowingly infringed.

The author would like to acknowledge the invaluable assistance given me by Cambridge University Press, and particularly Stephanie Boyd. I have been fortunate in the past four years to teach A-level students at Manshead School who have been critical both of my ideas and those of other historians and have made me rethink my views on the economic changes of the eighteenth and nineteenth centuries. I will always be grateful to them, especially Kate Doody and Sue Felstead, and to Graham Jenner (Head of Humanities) for their unwillingness to accept my 'tablets of stone'. The book is dedicated to my wife, Margaret, without whose support I would never have had the time to write.

Introduction

G.M. Trevelyan once suggested that historians should 'be conscious of our forefathers as they really were and, bit by bit, reconstruct the mosaic of the long forgotten past'. The changes that took place in the British economy in the eighteenth and early nineteenth centuries are both familiar and generally misunderstood. Familiar in their heroic dimensions with images of factories pouring out goods, chimneys polluting the air and landscape, exports expanding and productivity spiralling. Familiar too in the psychological characteristics they generated; these were, depending on your point of view, energy, inventiveness, courage and vigour, or shame, avarice, exploitation and cruelty. Familiar also in a focus on 'enterprise', of individual achievement and success, and on wealth creation in an unbridled market economy. Here is an epic drama, of Telfords, Stephensons and Darbys, Macadams, Brunels and Wedgwoods, a revolution not simply of inventions but also of the 'spirit'. But there is also misunderstanding. The 'dark satanic mills' were not all conquering. Individuals like Jethro Tull, James Hargreaves and Robert Bakewell, who to contemporaries personified 'improvement', have been reassessed and their central roles found to be the product of propagandists. Steam power, the personification of industrialisation, is now not seen either as pervasive or as significant as before. The importance of hand working and other traditional modes of production as late as 1850 has been stressed. To some 'industrial evolution' is a more accurate term to use than 'industrial revolution'.

Historians and sources

Historians

It is unfashionable among some economic historians today to regard the British economy, let alone any other economy, as having undergone an 'industrial revolution' between 1780 and 1840. However, the economic transformation of Britain was as deep-rooted, structural and overwhelming in its impact as the political revolution of 1789 in France. It is clear that some contemporaries, among them individuals with much practical experience in technology and manufactures, predicted, with hope, fear or satisfaction, the total transformation of society by means of industry: for example, in the aftermath of Waterloo the Tory Robert Southey and the socialist manufacturer Robert Owen [3.2]; Karl Marx [3.10] and Andrew Ure [3.22]; Friedrich Engels [3.5] and the scientist Charles Babbage.

The problem that historians have with the notion of an 'industrial revolution' lies in relation to the extent and speed of change. Are they using historical criteria, judging change relative to the experience of the past? Or comparing the experience of other economies and other regions at the time? Or are they looking at the changes retrospectively, judging them against later experience, whether of Britain or other industrialising countries? It is clear that many contemporaries from abroad, paying tribute to the dramatic novelty of steam engines and the factory system, or reflecting on the social visibility of places like Manchester or Bradford, were struck above all by the unlimited *potential* of the revolution they embodied, and the *speed* of the transformation they correctly predicted [2.3, 2.13, 3.1, 3.5]. Both modern sceptical historians and the prophetic contemporaries were right, yet they each concentrated on different aspects of reality. Historians stress the distance between 1830 and the 1990s, while contemporaries emphasised the lack of distance between 1830 and 1750 and what they saw as novel and dynamic rather than what remained from the past.

Sources

In *Change and Continuity in British Society 1800–1850*, a companion volume in this series, I outlined the problems historians face when examining the mass of sources available for this period. All sources have to be approached critically. Royal Commissions made up of 'experts' were often far from unbiased in their collection of evidence and reached preconceived conclusions. Witnesses examined before Select Committees could be unrepresentative in the views they expressed. Newspapers in the provinces took their news verbatim from London papers. Periodicals frequently put forward particular ideological positions. Social critics and commentators, often writing from a middle-class perspective, reflected an observed rather than an experienced assessment of the problems and behaviour of the working population. Visual sources claim an important place in this period. The physical landscape changed and was recorded in maps, prints, photographs and paintings and the remains of the 'industrial revolution' – factories, canals, railways, vast sprawling urban areas – can be interrogated.

The sources contained in this volume cover these areas. In approaching them it is important to consider the following questions:

1   Why were they *selected*? Presumably they have some significance for historians of economic change. What is that significance?
2   *Who* produced the source? Does the source reflect a direct observation of what was being discussed or was the information second-hand? Is it an honest expression of views or does it reflect a biased or prejudiced position? How have statistics been produced and for what reason?
3   *Why* was the source produced? Was it a deliberate decision or an unintended consequence of writing? If writing was deliberate is it possible to identify any 'hidden agenda' – does it support or attack a particular ideological position? Was it designed to defend or maintain a particular case? Historians need to adduce *motive* to those contemporaries whose evidence they rely upon.
4   For what *audience* was the source intended? The distinction between 'public' and 'private' audiences is important in evaluating sources. Are, for example, private communications likely to be more honest or more vitriolic than those written for public consumption?
5   How can historians *use* the source? How far does it exemplify a particular position? Is it of seminal importance in understanding the nature or significance of particular events? Is there other evidence to corroborate its use?

Historiography

The term 'industrial revolution' was coined by some French observers in the 1820s but did not enter common use in England until the 1880s, following the publication of Arnold Toynbee's lectures. Between 1890 and 1950 historians established a narrative and analytical framework for examining the industrial revolution through studying particular sectors of the economy, the development of inventions and the role of particular individuals. They also posed questions about whether change was beneficial or not and to whom. This marked the beginnings of the 'standard of living' debate. The industrial revolution, like so many other areas of economic history, has become increasingly studied through the use of economic theory and quantitative techniques. From the 1950s to the mid 1970s historians, stirred by the theories of development economists and buoyed up by the apparent success of the post-war welfare state, turned with vigour to Britain's industrial past. More recently, the industrial revolution has been scrutinised by the 'New Economic History' which emerged in the United States in the late 1950s. Old-fashioned historians were condemned for their unsystematic and unscientific marshalling of unreliable – because non-quantifiable – data.

The explosion of social history in the 1960s, a result in part of the narrowing of economic history, was not simply 'the history of the people with the politics left out', as Trevelyan would have us believe. It adopted a multi-disciplinary perspective, enlarged the map of historical knowledge and legitimated major new areas of scholarly enquiry – for example, the family, children, women, the ways ordinary people experienced and interacted with their developing economies. Understanding the role of change in the organisation of production, and hence in the organisation and experience of work, is central in understanding how and why the British economy developed between 1750 and 1850.

Cutting across explanations of economic change between 1750 and 1850 lies the question of whether the industrial revolution should be seen as a fundamental discontinuity in history and hence as a major turning point or not. In 1882 William Cunningham maintained that, 'Despite the gradual economic development, it seems likely though that, while centuries passed, there was little alteration in the general aspect of England; but the whole face of the country was changed by the Industrial Revolution . . .'. David Landes, one of the more recent exponents of the revolutionary approach, wrote in his *The Unbound Prometheus* in 1969 that, '[the industrial revolution] . . . marked a far more drastic break with the past than anything since the invention of the wheel'. For those who embrace discontinuity, the new industrialisation of the eighteenth century was both the precursor and essence of change. Individuals with different ideological slants nonetheless agree on discontinuity. Engels argued that the invention of the steam engine and the development of new machinery for manufacturing cotton in the second half of the eighteenth century brought the revolution. W.W. Rostow, in *The Stages of Economic Growth* (1960), which he subtitled 'A Non-Communist Manifesto', used the analogy of an aeroplane take-off to describe the crucial industrial breakthrough. Pre-industrial preparatory development might be substantial, even impressive, but in the context of the later revolution it remained essentially trivial.

The tradition of evolutionary growth has a pedigree almost as long as the revolutionary paradigm. Writing in 1890, the economist Marshall voiced a strong preference for an explanation in evolutionary terms, while much has been made of the failure of Sir John Clapham, in the inter-war period, to use the term 'industrial revolution' in any of his extensive writings. Lipson wrote in 1949 that 'If we destroy the legend that the inventions suddenly revolutionised English society and gave birth to a new industrial order we can at least put in its place a more rational interpretation in which the mechanical changes appear as a natural development in line with the course of historical evolution . . .'.

Approaches to understanding the changes that occurred in Britain between 1750 and 1850, whether from the 'revolutionary' or 'evolutionary' stables, are implicitly teleological. The 'goal' is basically the industrial structure that emerged at the height of Victorian prosperity and the threads of that structure are then sought in the past. The faltering of economic activity from the 1870s and the economic problems of the inter-war and post-war periods tend, as a result, to be discussed within the framework 'what happened to the industrial revolution?' rather than 'how is the recent economic structure to be explained?' 'Victorian values' do not, and, by their explicit 'pastness', cannot explain modern economic ills. We cannot replicate the 'industrial revolution'.

Growth

The meaning of growth

Historians concerned with the economic revolutions between 1750 and 1850 attempt to explain the process of economic development. But what do they mean by 'economic growth' and what were its major characteristics? The main indicator of long-term growth is the rate at which the income the country receives from goods and services, or Gross Domestic Product (GDP), increases. The data indicates a modest rate of growth during the eighteenth century, increasing from just under 1 per cent to just over it. In the first half of the nineteenth century growth remained at over 2 per cent. A better indicator of the advance of economic development is GDP per head of the population. Population growth was sufficient to sustain the growth process, but not so great as to swamp it in ways that Malthus feared. In the eighteenth and nineteenth centuries population grew at rather less than 1 per cent annually and was at least 1 per cent lower than the rate of growth of GDP.

There is some disagreement between historians about the timing of growth between 1750 and 1850:

Table showing British economic growth rates (per cent per annum)

	GDP	GDP/ head	Labour	Capital	Total factor productivity
1 Crafts					
1700–60	0.7	0.3	0.4	0.7	0.2
1760–80	0.7	0.0	0.7	0.8	0.1
1780–1801	1.3	0.4	1.0	1.2	0.4
1801–31	2.0	0.5	1.4	1.5	0.7
2 Feinstein					
1761–1800	1.1	0.3	0.8	1.0	0.2
1801–30	2.7	1.3	1.4	1.4	1.3
1831–60	2.5	1.1	1.4	2.0	0.8

From N.F.R. Crafts, 'British economic growth 1700–1831: a review of the evidence', *Economic History Review*, 2nd series, 36, (1983), pp. 187, 196; C.H. Feinstein, 'Capital formation in Great Britain', in P. Mathias and M.M. Postan (eds.), *Cambridge Economic History of Europe*, vol. VII, part I, Cambridge, 1978, p. 84

In broad terms the growth of GDP depends on three elements: an increase in labour, an increase in capital, and an increase in the productivity of these factors of production (called 'the total factor productivity'). The principal influence underlying the increase in labour was the growth of population in the eighteenth century. An increase in capital input, especially of fixed capital (buildings, machinery, etc.), represents a major prerequisite for any economic advance. This is clearly evident between 1760 and 1860.

Estimating productivity increase, known as total factor productivity, is far more contentious than estimates for capital and labour growth. Feinstein produces a higher estimate for the contribution of productivity than Crafts. Productivity is calculated by subtracting the rate of growth of labour and capital from the rate of growth of GDP. But, and this is the cause of disagreement, the growth rates of labour and capital must be weighted by their respective shares in national income. Different assumptions about the size of this share produced different patterns in the allocation of GDP growth between labour, capital and productivity. Crafts, for example, allows a 15 per cent share to land, a not unreasonable assumption, which leaves a larger productivity than if the more conventional division between capital and labour is adopted. Other assumptions about the size of factor shares produce quite different patterns in the allocation of GDP growth between labour, capital and productivity.

It is important to recognise, as the brief discussion of productivity exemplifies, that though historians may agree on what economic factors contribute to economic growth, how the relationship between those factors is interpreted is open to question. The remainder of the Introduction will attempt to draw some conclusions from the analyses of revisionist historians on growth, perspective and causation.

Identifying and explaining growth

In 1962 Deane and Cole published their *British Economic Growth 1688–1959*. It offered new estimates of the overall rate of economic growth and of changes in the structure of economic activity, the two main criteria which are central to the definition of the 'industrial revolution'. Much of the early use and discussion of Deane and Cole's work was related to the 'stages' theory of economic growth advanced by W.W. Rostow in 1960. He argued that the British economy experienced a 'take-off into self-sustained growth' in the period 1783–1802. This 'take-off' marked a 'decisive transition' involving sharp rises in the share of the country's resources allocated to investment and the emergence of leading sectors (cotton and iron) which exerted a fundamental influence over growth as a whole. Rostow also suggested that this British experience was the prototype for all other industrialised countries.

Rostow's hypothesis was not given much support by the Deane and Cole estimates which suggested a more gradualist interpretation – change in slow motion – of overall growth as a basis for the dramatic, though not dominant, developments in iron and cotton production; and they indicated that the rise in investment was quite modest relative to the increase in total output.

Deane and Cole provided the starting point for important revisions of the statistical record, of which those by N.F.R. Crafts in *British Economic Growth during the Industrial Revolution* (1985) are the most recent and best tested. However, the surge of economic growth associated with the industrial revolution came as a surprise to many contemporaries who were more impressed by the constraints on growth rather than by the opportunities for expansion. This intriguing paradox is explored by E.A. Wrigley in his *Continuity, Chance and Change: The Character of the Industrial Revolution in England* (1988). He argues that classical economists doubted the possibility of sustained economic growth because of the nature of pre-industrial economies entirely dependent on organic raw materials, inhibited by the very limited scale of available heat and mechanical energy and faced with the seeming inevitability of declining productivity. The period down to the early nineteenth century is regarded by Wrigley as a period in which the sources of growth were mainly those of an advanced organic economy. After this the mineral-based energy economy became increasingly dominant as a vehicle of growth.

The nature of the advanced organic economy is depicted clearly in the writings of the classical economists. Within the economic system they constructed the opportunities for growth were very substantial yet firmly limited. Growth was inescapably limited because one of the three factors – land, labour and capital – upon whose combination all production depended, was in fixed supply. Land could not be increased and as a result the limited marginal returns in agriculture, though capable of postponement, could not in the long run be avoided. The recognition of the significance of the productivity of the land to a whole range of productive activities is explicit in the writings of classical economists. It was Malthus who brought this aspect of the matter most vividly into focus in his *An Essay on the Principle of Population*. It is an implicit assumption of his writings that the constraints imposed by a universal dependence on organic raw materials were severe and permanent. Unless fertility was controlled the inevitable result would be declining productivity, standards of living and growth prospects.

To escape these constraints, it was necessary to find alternatives for animal and vegetable raw materials in production processes which did not suffer from the same disadvantage. The central feature of the mineral-based energy economy, according to Wrigley, was its ability to free production from dependence on the productivity of the land. The use of organic raw materials was much reduced in long-established branches of industry and major new sectors of industry were opened up in which the consumption of organic materials played little or no part. The advent of the new system allowed the application of heat and mechanical energy in productive processes on a scale without earlier parallel. The existing constraints on the scale of output ended, unit production costs declined continuously across a wide range of industries and both productivity and production could rise without threatening a subsistence crisis. Output could outstrip population; production could distance reproduction. There was now sufficient productive capacity to meet all basic human needs with a substantial margin to spare. The issue ceased to be one of subsistence but of whether economic capacity was being properly used.

The transition from an advanced organic to an energy-based mineral economy was long drawn-out. Mineral sources of energy began to replace alternatives as early as the late sixteenth century. But, as will be seen in Chapter 3 (page 57) where the debate on proto-industrialisation is considered, productivity increases were not closely linked to the use of new sources of mechanical energy which were still affecting only a small fraction of the labour force by the mid 1830s. Viewed in this way the century between 1750 and 1850 was one of some uncertainty. The behaviour of real income per head, one of the key defining indicators of an industrial revolution, had risen between 1650 and 1750 because of the benefits of an increasingly efficient organic economy. But for the next century its path was uncertain overall. For workers firmly rooted in the organic economy, especially in agriculture in southern and eastern England, movement was probably downwards. For those affected by the development of the mineral-based economy there may have been advance, though the regional situation is complicated by the slow decline of the domestic industry.

What then are the key features of the new view on economic growth in the eighteenth and early nineteenth centuries for historians? Recent research can be summarised as follows.

1 Between 1760 and 1840 the British economy experienced a very rapid and, by international standards, pronounced structural change. The proportion of the labour force employed in industry, whether in the 'secondary' or 'tertiary' sectors, increased, and the proportion employed in farming fell very rapidly.

2 However, much of the employment in industry continued to be in small-scale, handicraft activities producing for local markets. These trades were hardly affected by new technology and so experienced little or no increase in output per worker. Where there was an increase in productivity it was achieved by getting more workers into the industry.

3 The experience of cotton textile production, though dynamic and of high contemporary profile, was not typical and there was no general triumph of steam power or the factory system in the early nineteenth century, nor was economic growth raised spectacularly by a few decisive innovations.

4 The acceleration in the overall pace of economic growth was perceptible but modest. There was no great leap forward for the economy as a whole, despite the experience of cotton textile production.

5 By 1850 Britain was labelled the 'workshop of the world' and the advance in productivity in a few industries did enable Britain to sell around half of all world trade in manufacture. This, however, needs to be seen in the context of the main feature of British industrialisation: the 'industrial revolution' involved getting more workers into the industrial sector rather than achieving higher output per worker once they were there. The cotton and iron industries coexisted with other industries characterised by low productivity, low pay and low levels of exports.

If the notion of an 'industrial revolution' is increasingly seen as a 'metaphor' for the changes that occurred in the British economy then perhaps D. McCloskey is right to argue that 'The cure for excess in metaphor is counting.' The result of the work of the 'New Economic History' has been the creation of a new perspective on economic change in this period, a rewriting of the 'industrial revolution' to emphasise the slowness and unevenness of growth, the relatively slow diffusion of the new technology and of factory production [3.16] and the rejection of any sudden or 'revolutionary' break with the past. For the moment, at least, 'change in slow motion' has replaced the 'unbound Prometheus'.

A question of perspective

How far is it possible to see the economic changes that occurred between 1750 and 1850 in their 'total' setting? One criticism of the quantitative approach to history is that, as the French historian Georges Lefebvre ruefully commented, 'living, suffering man does not appear in it'. Statistical evidence, though of obvious importance, only provides historians with trends and tendencies. The changes that occurred did not just happen, they happened to people who acted, reacted, opposed or supported those changes in different ways. The result has been studies of economic change which focus on particular sectors of the economy or on particular regions or localities.

The issue is highlighted when the question of national perspectives is considered. England, Wales, Scotland and Ireland had contrasting experiences between 1750 and 1850, a consequence of different resources, climate, societies, cultures and histories. Yet most studies of British economic change have England and, to a lesser extent, Wales as their focal points. Developments in Scotland, Wales and Ireland are used to illustrate points relevant to England's experience rather than as examples of changing economies in their own right. The result of this has been that the English perspective has been accepted as the 'norm'. This has important effects in three respects:

1   There is a failure to establish any meaningful dialogue between the English experience and that of the other countries
2   It perpetuates myths about the economic nature of Scotland, Wales and Ireland and of their peoples
3   It means that *British* history actually means *English* history.

So how does examining issues from a broader perspective help in understanding the process of economic change between 1750 and 1850? Take, for example, demographic growth. Why has English growth been considered the norm for demographic analysis? The problem with the available evidence provides part of the answer. In England parish registers are available for almost all parishes but in Wales only about a third have survived, and in Scotland and Ireland the figure is much lower. Yet examination of the chronology of population change between 1700 and 1850 in the four areas shows marked differences. The populations of both Ireland and Scotland grew at faster rates than England's between 1700 and 1750. England's rate of growth of 0.7 per cent per year between 1750 and 1800 was lower than Ireland's. Scotland's population revolution did not really begin till after 1800 when Ireland's had lost its momentum. Differences in general trends are borne out by looking at particular reasons for growth. The introduction of the potato in Ireland, but also in Highland Scotland, arguably had an impact on birth rates. Did it remove the constraints which had previously held population down? Why were prenuptially conceived births lower in Ireland than in England and Wales but highest in Scotland? With all these differences, the impact of, and reasons for, population growth need to be evaluated more carefully. The formula that

population growth = growing demand = stimulus to economic growth

is an oversimplification. Ireland did not undergo dramatic economic change between 1750 and 1800 when its population expanded, while Scotland's burst of industrial activity from the 1770s predated its population growth by twenty years.

The question of causation

Why did the economic changes occur? Answers to this question usually focus on why the cotton, iron and coal industries expanded and what impact the diffusion of steam power had. Important though these areas undoubtedly were, they neglect the broader economic experiences of Britain between 1750 and 1850. Similarly the question 'Why did the industrial revolution occur in Britain rather than France or the Netherlands or Germany?' often misses the crucial point that economic changes did not occur in Britain *as a whole* but in particular areas like Lancashire, the Central Lowlands of Scotland, South Wales or around Belfast, and that there was no necessary connection between developments in one area and those in others. Recognition of the regional nature of economic change or decline is important but it only has value when considered in terms of contributions to national trends. Attempts to find a 'leading sector' – was it population growth or increased domestic demand or technological change which led to the industrial revolution? – again seems to miss the point.

Explaining why changes occurred in the economy is extremely difficult since economic developments had an effect, however small, on all aspects of society. Some circumstances that were present in Britain facilitated change and, in that sense, can be said to be causal. Others impeded progress but change occurred despite them. It is in their impact on people, the living-through of economic changes, that the importance of the 'industrial revolution' lies rather than in the search for an all-embracing explanation of why it occurred.

Conclusion

This introduction contains little that has traditionally been associated with the industrial revolution. There is no description of the emergence of the mechanised cotton industry, the labour-intensive coal industry, the promethean iron industry or the energy revolution associated with James Watt and the steam engine. The view of there even being an industrial 'revolution' is questioned though it would be perverse to refrain from using a term 'hallowed by usage'. Yet even in the traditional view change in slow motion is implicit: Watt was preceded by Newcomen, changes in the iron industry lasted from Abraham Darby in the early eighteenth century to James Neilson in the late 1820s and the mechanisation of cotton took at least fifty years. It may be possible to demonstrate, by evidence and equation, that change occurred slowly between 1750 and 1850 but it is of fundamental importance to understand that many people saw themselves as living through or having lived through an era of revolution – a process of transformation that was convulsing Britain and its society. Without that understanding it is difficult to appreciate either economic change or continuity. Developments in the economy may be incremental, piecemeal or planned. They may create or destroy, be opposed or supported but they are not inevitable.

1 A revolution in numbers

If it is possible to identify a single cause for the economic revolutions that occurred between 1750 and 1850 – something on which there is considerable debate among historians – then perhaps the best case can be made for the dramatic increase in the population of the British Isles. This certainly led to a rise in demand for subsistence goods like food and housing. But the increase in demand for other goods – more manufactured goods or more efficient means of communication – did not necessarily follow from population expansion. Yet on this central development in British history there is still much disagreement. Was it caused by changes in the fertility rate, or the mortality rate, or a combination of the two? What impact did the age of marriage have? Did demographic expansion in Scotland and Ireland follow developments in England and Wales? This chapter will examine three aspects of this revolution in numbers. First, the controversy of the second half of the eighteenth century over whether population was rising or falling will be examined. This will be followed by a section in which statistical data for population change and reasons for rising fertility will be considered. Finally, the Irish Famine of the 1840s and the fragility of demographic growth will be discussed.

The population controversy

In the second edition of his *Observations on Reversionary Payments*, published in 1772, Richard Price suggested that 'in this kingdom, it appears that, amidst all our splendour, we are decreasing so fast, as to have lost, in about 70 years, near a quarter of our people'. By contrast, Horace Walpole wrote in a letter to Mary Berry in 1791, though only of London, that:

There will soon be one street from London to Brentford; ay, and from London to every village ten miles around! . . . nor do I wonder; London is, I am certain, much fuller than ever I saw it. I have twice this spring been going to stop my coach in Piccadily, to inquire what was the matter, thinking there was a mob – not at all; it was only passengers.

Why was there such fundamental disagreement among contemporaries and what form did that disagreement take?

George Grenville, Prime Minister in the mid 1760s, and William Thornton, an MP, debated the necessity for a census in 1753.

For and against a census: the 1753 Parliamentary debate

1.1   George Grenville

[A census], it is said, can answer no purpose but that of an insignificant and vain curiosity, as if it were of no consequence for the legislature to know when to encourage and when to discourage or restrain the people of this island, or of some particular part of it, from going to settle in our American Colonies. Do gentlemen think, that it can be of no use to this society . . . to know when the number of its people increases or decreases; and when the latter appears to be the case, to enquire into the cause of it and to endeavour to employ a proper remedy . . . ? Even here at home do we not know, that both manufactures and the number of people have in late years decreased in some parts of the Kingdom? Would it not be of advantage to us to know, whether this affects the whole, or if it be only on removal from one part of the island to another? . . .

Hansard, 26 George II, debate in the Commons on the Bill for Registering the Number of People, 8 May 1753, pp. 1350–1

1.2   William Thornton

It has been said, Sir, that an authentic knowledge of the number of our people, and of their annual increase or decrease, will instruct us when to encourage, and when to restrain people from going to settle in our American Colonies. Sir, our going or not going to America does not depend upon the public encouragement or restraint, but upon the circumstances they are in at the time. Let the number of our people be never so much increased, those who can easily find the means of subsistence at home neither will go, nor ought we to encourage them to go to America; and let that number be never so much diminished, we ought not to restrain those from going thither who can find no way of subsisting at home . . .

Ibid., pp. 1355–6

Questions

1 What was the basis of Grenville's support for and of Thornton's opposition to an annual census of England and Wales?
2 Why did Grenville maintain that it was essential to know whether population was increasing or not?

3 Why do you think the parliamentary debates on the 1753 Bill generated such depth of feeling?
4 How could the suspicion of censuses as a tool of government policy and an infringement on personal liberties have been expressed by both supporters and opponents of the 1753 Bill?

The 1753 Bill was hotly debated and passed the House of Commons only to fall in the Lords. The result was a controversy which lasted until the Bill for taking the 1801 census was being discussed. Writers were hampered by both the lack of reliable statistics and their own personal limitations. The first phase of the debate began in the mid 1750s with disagreements between William Brakenridge, Rector of St Michael Bassishaw, London, and Richard Forster, Rector of Great Shefford, Berkshire. The second stage attracted more attention partly because it was initiated by Dr Richard Price, one of the major writers of the century, and lasted throughout the 1770s.

1.3   William Brakenridge

[The London Bills of Mortality] plainly shews that the inhabitants were increasing till about the year 1728; and that from thence to 1743, they remained in the same state nearly; but that afterwards, during the last ten years, till 1753, they were constantly diminishing. For it is evident that the number of inhabitants must always be in proportion to the number of births, and burials considered together.

'A letter from the Reverend William Brakenridge, D.D. and F.R.S. to George Lewis Scot, Esq., F.R.S., concerning the Number of Inhabitants within the London Bills of Mortality', *Philosophical Transactions*, vol. 48, II, 1755, no. XCV, pp. 788–800

1.4   Richard Forster

That it was plain matter of fact, that England is more Populous, rich & powerfull, since it planted Colonies, than it was before. It having been found by Experience, as well as by Calculation, that Every Man Employed as He ought to be in America finds Employment for 4 pairs of Hands in Old England. So that Every one, who is lost to us by Emigrating to our Plantations, is ye Cause of three being gain'd to us upon ye real Balance . . .

Letter to Thomas Birch, 2 December 1760, Birch MSS. 4440, no. 176, printed in full in D.V. Glass, *Numbering the People*, 1973, pp. 78–89

1.5a   Richard Price: a nephew comments

The increasing burthens which oppressed the poor, together with the growing luxury and extravagance which pervaded the higher ranks of society, were, in his opinion, making dreadful inroads into the population of the Kingdom . . .

William Morgan, *Memoirs of the Life of Richard Price, D.D., F.R.S.,* London, 1815, pp. 85–6

1.5b   Richard Price's view

I have observed that London is now increasing. But it appears that, in truth, this is an event more to be dreaded than desired. The more London increases, the more the rest of the Kingdom must be deserted: the fewer hands must be left in agriculture; and, consequently, the less must be the plenty and the higher the prices of all the means of subsistence. Moderate towns, being seats of refinement, emulation and arts, may be public advantages. But great towns, long before they grow to half the bulk of London, become checks on population of too hurtful a nature, nurseries of debauchery and voluptuousness; and in many respects, greater evils than can be compensated for by any advantage.

Richard Price, 'Observations on the Expectations of Lives, the Increase of Mankind . . .', *Philosophical Transactions*, vol. 59, 1769, pp. 118–19

1.6a   Arthur Young attacks statistical calculations

The calculations drawn up from the number of houses are, in all probability, fallacious: that they are mere guesses we well know; for by what rule is the number of souls per house to be determined? How is the medium to be found out between the palace and the cot? . . . Besides, how are we to know that the number per house is always the same?

A. Young, *Proposals to the Legislature for Numbering the People,* London, 1771, pp. 4–6

1.6b

All guesses at the number of people are fallacious. There are no data sufficient for the calculation. Besides, depopulation is the fashion with a set of men who wish to decry the state of the nation; and they have found writers visionary enough, from very fallible materials, to pronounce, with an authoritative air, that we are not four million and an half.

A. Young, *Political Arithmetic*, Part 2, London, 1779, p. 25

1.7   John Howlett attacks Price

[great towns were] indications or causes of greater advantage . . . the natural concomitants of overflowing wealth, of extensive manufactures, of wide and flourishing commerce . . . there cannot a doubt remain that our population has almost doubled [since 1688].

J. Howlett, *An Examination of Dr Price's Essay*, Maidstone, 1781, pp. 9, 129

1.8   Charles Abbot speaks in the Commons in 1800

[It is necessary] to substitute certainty for conjecture and instead of approximation have the fact . . . by showing the increase or diminution of baptisms, burials and marriages, from the latter of which, I mean the marriages of which the registers are much more comprehensive, complete and important, we shall have a correct knowledge of what concerns our increasing or decreasing demands for subsistence.

Hansard's *Parliamentary History*, vol. 35, cols. 598–602

1.9   A historian comments

The eighteenth-century political arithmeticians of England made no advances whatsoever upon the position reached by Graunt, Petty and King. They were second-rate imitators of men of genius.

M. Greenwood, *Medical Statistics from Graunt to Farr*, Cambridge, 1948, p. 49

Questions

1   What were the basic arguments employed in the debate on population in the 1750s and the 1770s and 1780s?

2   What, from the point of view of modern historians, were the weaknesses in the methods employed in calculating population totals by those arguing for population decline?

3   Oliver Goldsmith in the preface to his poem 'The Deserted Village', first published in 1769, wrote: 'In regretting the depopulation of the country, I inveigh against the increases in our luxuries . . .'. What evidence is there in sources 1.3–1.8 that depopulation was attributed to urban growth? In what ways does this evidence rely on a moral perspective rather than economic arguments?

4   What specific circumstances in the 1790s meant that Charles Abbot successfully supported demands for a census?

5 Comment on the validity of Greenwood's statement [1.9] with reference to the previous documents in the chapter.
6 'The contemporary demographic debate adds little to historians' understanding of population change in the eighteenth century.' Discuss.

A question of statistics

Why did Britain's population rise between 1750 and 1850? There may be a simple answer to this question – population rose because births exceeded deaths, but the causes of rising birth rates, the reasons for declining death rates and their precise chronologies are far more difficult to resolve.

Pre-1801 population figures are calculated by historians using material from parish registers and other contemporary sources.

1.10   Table showing population growth (in millions)

Date	England	England and Wales	Scotland	Ireland
1701	5.06	5.30	1.04	2.54
1751	5.77	6.50	1.25	3.12
1761	6.15	6.70	—	—
1771	6.45	7.20	—	—
1781	7.04	7.50	—	—
1791	7.74	8.25	1.50	4.75
1801	8.66	9.20	1.60	5.22
1811	9.89	10.20	1.80	6.00
1821	11.49	12.00	2.10	6.80
1831	13.28	13.90	2.40	7.80
1841	14.97	15.90	2.60	8.20
1851	16.74	17.90	2.90	6.50

The figures for England, excluding Monmouthshire, are from E.A. Wrigley and R.S. Schofield, *The Population History of England 1541–1871: A Reconstitution*, London, 1981, Cambridge, 1989, pp. 528–9. Other material is from P. Deane and W.A. Cole, *British Economic Growth 1688–1959*, Cambridge, 1969, p. 6

1.11 Table showing population growth rates (as annual percentages)

Country	1700–1750	1750–1800	1800–1850
England and Wales	0.3	0.8	1.8
Scotland	0.6	0.5	1.6
Ireland	0.6	1.1	0.6

From N. Tranter, *Population since the Industrial Revolution*, 1973, p. 43, and E.A. Wrigley and R.S. Schofield, *The Population History of England 1541–1871: A Reconstitution*, 1989, pp. 528–9

1.12 Table showing births and deaths per thousand for England (excluding Monmouthshire)

Year	Birth rate	Death rate
1701	34.2	26.7
1751	34.2	26.3
1761	34.8	26.5
1771	35.2	27.2
1781	35.5	29.7
1791	38.4	25.4
1801	33.9	28.1
1811	40.0	26.5
1821	40.9	23.4
1831	35.2	22.5
1841	36.0	22.0
1851	36.4	22.1

E.A. Wrigley and R.S. Schofield, *The Population History of England 1541–1871: A Reconstitution*, 1989., pp. 533–5

1.13 Table showing the mean age of first marriage in England 1700–1850

Period	Male	Female
1700–49	28.1	27.0
1750–99	27.1	25.4
1800–49	26.5	24.3

From E.A. Wrigley, 'Age of Marriage in Early Modern England', unpublished paper quoted in R. Floud and D. McCloskey (eds.), *The Economic History of Britain since 1700*, vol. 1: *1700–1860*, 1981, p. 27

Questions

1 Using sources 1.10–1.13 describe the demographic development of England and the remainder of the British Isles between 1700 and 1850.
2 What might be the causal link between source 1.13 and the birth rates in source 1.12? Is this sufficient to explain growing population? Explain your answer fully.
3 What questions are raised by these statistics which need further explanation?
4 Historians have developed the notion of 'the long eighteenth century'. What does this mean and how do these sources demonstrate its validity?
5 England's demographic growth in this period has often been taken as the norm for growth in the British Isles. How has this distorted our understanding of population trends?

Population and economic growth

The total population of a given area and its distribution is the result of the interaction between fertility and mortality rates, immigration and emigration and internal migration. Recent research has placed legitimate and illegitimate fertility at the centre of explanations and that there was a correlation between it and trends in economic conditions. Wrigley and Schofield argue that children born in the relative prosperity of 1725–50, when employment opportunities and real wages were high, were inclined to marry earlier in the third quarter of the century despite less conducive economic conditions. This 'delayed-response' meant that fertility declined between the 1810s and 1830s, while the higher real wages of the 1800s led to higher fertility after 1835. How far is there a positive correlation between incomes and fertility?

1.14   Arthur Young

Why have the inhabitants of Birmingham increased from 23,000 in 1750 to 30,000 in 1770? Certainly because a proportional increase in employment has taken place; wherever there is a demand for hands, there they will abound . . . Thus where employment increases, the people increase; and where employment does not increase the people do not increase . . . Away my boys – get children, they are worth more than they ever were.

A. Young, *Political Arithmetic*, London, 1774, p. 61

1.15   Adam Smith

But poverty, though it does not prevent the generation, is extremely unfavourable to the rearing of children. The tender plant is produced but in so cold a soil and so severe a climate, it soon withers and dies. It is not uncommon, I have been frequently told, in the Highlands of Scotland for a mother who has borne twenty children not to have two alive . . . The liberal reward of labour, by enabling them to produce better for their children, and consequently to bring up a greater number, naturally tends to widen and extend those limits. It deserves to be remarked too, that it necessarily does this as nearly as possible in the proportion which the demand for labour requires. If this demand is continually increasing, the reward of labour must necessarily encourage in such a manner that marriage and multiplication of labourers, as may enable them to supply that continually increasing demand by a continually increasing population.

Adam Smith, *An Inquiry into the Nature and Causes of the Wealth of Nations*, book 1, London, 1776, edited by A. Skinner, 1970, pp. 182–3

1.16   Thomas Malthus

Little or no doubt can exist that the comforts of the labouring poor depend upon the increase of the fund destined for the maintenance of labour, and will be very exactly in proportion to the rapidity of this increase. The demand for labour which such increases would occasion, by creating a competition in the market, must necessarily raise the value of labour, and, till the additional number of hands required were reared, the increased funds would be distributed to the same number of people as before the increase, and therefore every labourer would live comparatively at his ease. But perhaps Dr Adam Smith errs in representing every increase of the revenue or stock of a society as an increase of these funds . . . A distinction will in this case occur, between the number of hands which the stock of the society could employ, and the number which its territory can maintain.

T.R. Malthus, *An Essay on the Principle of Population*, London, 1798, edited by A. Flew, 1970, pp. 183–4

1.17   A later comment

The industrial and agricultural revolutions carried with them a shift from settled, traditional ways of life, in which changes came slowly, to new ways of life in which changes were liable to be frequent and abrupt. The old settled ways of life, in which ties of family and community had been strong . . . were passing. They were succeeded by an intense competitive struggle in which the emphasis was placed on the individual rather than the community. Opportunities for 'getting on' were multiplied, but, at the same time, it became increasingly necessary to struggle to keep one's job and one's place in the community . . .

***Royal Commission on Population*, London, 1949, p. 39**

Questions

1 In what ways is the Wrigley and Schofield 'delayed-response' thesis supported by sources 1.10–1.13?
2 What arguments about population growth do Arthur Young [1.14] and Adam Smith [1.15] put forward?
3 In what ways does Malthus [1.16] disagree with Young and Smith? Why is there disagreement?
4 How do sources 1.1–1.8 support the thesis put forward by Adam Smith?
5 What is the value of 1.17 in attempting to explain why population rose and what its effects were?
6 'Demographic expansion can simply be explained by economic expansion.' Discuss.

Famine in Ireland

There is no doubting the fragility of life in subsistence economies as the famines of the 1980s have made all too clear. Uncontrolled population growth is accompanied, for Malthusian reasons if no others, by periodic reversals. Subsistence crises, often expressed in food riots, were a part of population expansion between 1700 and 1850 but it is the scale of the 'Great Hunger' in Ireland between 1845 and 1850 that occasioned so much contemporary comment and subsequent historians' interest. The final section of this chapter places famine in Ireland in a broader historical context. William Wilde, a young Irish surgeon who had collected and collated data on mortality for the 1851 Irish census, produced a table of Irish famines from 900 to 1850. Though there are defects in its survey, for example, there is no mention of a severe famine in 1629, Wilde used a wide array of sources.

1.18 Wilde's plan

In recording the fact, as well as analysing, the extent, causes and concomitants of the recent 'plague, pestilence and famine', with which it has pleased Providence to afflict this country, we naturally looked back to native history for parallels . . . we perceive that so far as the annals and records of the country afford information, Ireland has from the earliest period of its colonisation to the present time been subjected to a series of dire calamities, affecting human life, arising either from causes originating within itself, or from its connexion with Great Britain and other parts of Europe.

The Census of Ireland for the Year 1851, part V, *Tables of Deaths*, vol. I, *British Parliamentary Papers*, 1856, XXIX, p. 2

1.19 Wilde's Table of Irish Famines

Year: 1739
Event and circumstance: 'In the beginning of November 1739 we had a very sharp, cold, N.E. wind, and which continued for about three weeks; this succeeded in the severest frost known here in the memory of man, which entirely destroyed the potatoes, the chief support of the poor . . .'
Authority: Sylvester O'Halloran, *Treatise on the Air*, manuscript, Royal Irish Academy

Year: 1739
Event and circumstance: 'At the conclusion of the year 1739, there happened an exceeding cold winter . . . From this dreadful and indescribably hard frost, there arose shortly afterwards not only a great destruction of all sorts of cattle but a lamentable blight . . . [of] those tuberous roots (commonly called potatoes), almost the continual and sole food of the poor and lower orders of this kingdom . . .'
Authority: Maurice O'Connell, *Morborum Acutorum et Chronicorum quorundam Observationes Medicales Experimentales* . . . , Dublin, 1746

Year: 1741
Event and circumstance: 'It was computed that as many people [400,000] died of want and disorders occasioned by it, during that time, as fell by the sword in the rebellion of 1641. Whole parishes were almost desolate, and the dead were eaten in the fields by dogs, for want of people to bury them'.
Authority: Philip Skelton, *The Necessity of Tillage and Granaries* . . . , Dublin, 1741

Year: 1801
Event and circumstance: 'POTATO FAILURE. – The summer of 1801 proved remarkably dry and hot in Ireland, vegetation was obstructed, Potatoes failed, and a famine was near taking place among the poor, whose chief food in Ireland is potatoes.'
Authority: *Transactions of the Royal Dublin Society*, 1801

Year: 1821
Event and circumstance: 'All the newspapers of the time agree as to the fact of the unparalleled wetness of the autumn, which had the effect of souring the potato, even then of stunted growth . . . This peculiar failure of the potato crop, which was almost confined to certain districts of the west and south, was the manifest product of a want of balance . . . The cereal crops of Ireland were not at all injured in proportion . . .
Authority: C.E. Trevelyan, *The Irish Crisis*, London, 1848

Year: 1845
Event and circumstance: The potato disease is manifest in Sligo, Mayo and Galway. We admit with inexpressible reluctance that constant proofs which we receive of the wide extent to which the potato disease has reached. We are unlikely to believe that famine is likely to afflict us – but it is now as impossible as it would be criminal to suppress the fact that the pestilence has spread far and wide, and has invaded our own and the neighbouring counties, which we fondly hoped were wholly safe . . .'
Authority: Saunders' News-Letter, *Cork Southern Reporter*

Year: 1846
Event and circumstance: 'Before the end of the year the poor cottiers and labourers were utterly destitute. The calamity fell with peculiar severity on the farm servants; these were among the first victims of starvation. The price of food rose enormously: turnips were sold at 1s. to 1s. 6d. per cwt. Want and misery spread throughout the land; disease rapidly followed . . . '
Authority: J. Pim, *Condition and Prospect of Ireland,* **Dublin, 1848**

Year: 1847
Event and circumstance: 'In the third year the disease had nearly exhausted itself, but it still appeared in different parts of the country. Although the potatoes sown . . . were estimated at only one-fifth or one-sixth of the usual quantity, it would have been a serious aggravation of the difficulties and discouragements under which that portion of the empire was suffering, if the disease had re-appeared in its unmitigated form . . . '
Authority: C.E. Trevelyan, *The Irish Crisis,* **London, 1848**

Year: 1849
Event and circumstance: 'The potatoes last year were almost universally blighted; and the late-sown crop never came to perfection at all. These wet and unripe potatoes being unfit for food were kept for seed; and the crop of this year proved weak and unhealthy, and even in May exhibited the blight on the leaves, which broke into holes.'
Authority: *Irish Farmer's Gazette*

This selection is based on the more extensive table printed in E. Margaret Crawford (ed.), *Famine: The Irish Experience 900–1900,* **Edinburgh, 1989, pp. 3–30**

1.20   Images: a historian's perception

That Irish image was, from the 1840s, both dominated and epitomized by the famine, a catastrophe that did enormous (and it could be argued, ultimately fatal) damage to the Union relationship. It provided Irish nationalists with material for a most fundamental and emotional indictment of England – the charge that it contrived the extermination and banishment of the Irish on the scale of mass murder. The reality was that the famine revealed the blind rigidities of English policy and the gross inadequacy of English economic orthodoxy . . . even more was it simply a disaster beyond all expectation and imagination. But the image which grew, fed by these grievous shortcomings, was one of genocide: ' . . . that million and a half men, women and children were carefully, prudently, and peacefully slain by the English government' – this was to be an enduring nationalist theme, voiced most bitterly and most vehemently in the widely popular histories of John Mitchel.

P. O'Farrell, *England and Ireland since 1800*, Oxford, 1975, p. 29

Questions

1 What do you think Wilde's intention was in producing this table? Do you think he succeeded in this and why?
2 What information does this selection from Wilde contain about the incidence of famines affecting potatoes before 1845?
3 The potato was central to the Irish diet. Why was this the case and what problems did it create?
4 The Famine was only one demographic crisis among many, so why has it become such an emotive issue in Ireland?
5 What were the major demographic and economic consequences of the Famine?
6 Why did famine between 1700 and 1850 occur with such devastating results in Ireland but not in England?

The growing populations of England, Wales, Scotland and Ireland provided a major impetus to economic change after 1750. The economic revolutions effectively broke through the restraints on change that population growth had always previously exerted – the central fear of Malthus. Unrestrained growth of population could lead to subsistence crises, or in the case of Ireland, full-blown famine. But population expansion stimulated an urban explosion with its associated environmental and health problems. It created a 'mass' society ultimately grounded in the 'mass' workplace of the factory with its 'mass' meetings of trade unionism, 'mass' political parties and its 'mass' media. Growth was an ambiguous phenomenon.

2 Revolutions on the land

Agriculture dominated economic life for over 10,000 years and until the early nineteenth century a large proportion of Britain's population was directly employed in farming and pastoral activities or in providing raw materials for industry. Despite the relative sophistication of the British economy in the eighteenth century and the growing impetus towards manufacturing industry in the early nineteenth century, people who worked in agriculture made up the largest occupational group in the 1851 census. Historians have seen the 'agricultural revolution' as a cause and result of both demographic and industrial change. Yet the processes of agricultural change are slow and recently the origins of the transformation of British farming have been pushed back into the seventeenth century. So can historians still talk about a 'revolution' in farming and what does 'revolution' mean in this context?

This chapter focuses on change in farming in four respects: the nature of agricultural improvement as seen by Arthur Young between 1770 and 1810; secondly, the rationalisation of land through enclosure; thirdly, the impact of change on output. The chapter will end with an examination of how change was perceived by contemporary novelists and poets.

A dynamic economy?

Increased output in farming was achieved by making the land more productive and by bringing more land into arable or pastoral use. New crops and new rotations were well established when the proliferation of parliamentary enclosures, seen by some historians as marking the 'classical' agricultural revolution, began in the 1760s. How dynamic was the rural economy before 1760? In 1700 Richard Gough wrote of Myddle, a village community in Shropshire:

2.1 Long-term improvement

This William Watkin was a person well educated, and fitt for greater employment than that of a husbandman . . . Hee found this farme much overgrowne with thornes, briars and rubish. Hee imployd many day labourers (to whom he was a good benefactor) in cleareing and ridding his land; and having the benefitt of good marle, he much improved his land, built part of the dwelling house, and joined the brewhouse to it, which hee built of free stone. Hee built most part of the barnes and made beast houses of free stone, which is a good substantial piece of building . . . [his grandson] William Watkin is now owner of this farme, and very happy in that it hath pleased God to give him such skill, care and industry in good husbandry as his grand-father and father had, for hee is not inferiour to eyther of them therein.

Richard Gough, *The History of Myddle*, edited by D. Hey, 1981, pp. 111, 114

Twenty-five years later Daniel Defoe wrote:

2.2 A thriving countryside

From hence, crossing still the roads leading from London into Sussex, keeping on [east] we come to Westerham, the first market town in Kent on that side. This is a neat handsome well built market-town, and is full of gentry, and consequently of good company. All this part of the country is very agreeably pleasant, wholesome and fruitful, I mean quite from Guildford to this place; and is accordingly overspread with good towns, gentlemen's houses, populous villages, abundance of fruit, with hop-grounds and cherry orchards, and the lands well cultivated; but all on the right-hand, that is to say, south is exceedingly grown with timber, has abundance of waste and wild grounds, and forests, and woods, with many large iron works, at which they cast great quantities of iron cauldrons, chimney-backs, furnaces, retorts, boiling pots and all such necessary things of iron . . . though at the same time the works are prodigiously expensive, and the quantity of wood they consume is exceeding great, which keeps up that complaint I mentioned before that timber would grow scarce, and consequently dear, from the great quantity consumed in the iron-works in Sussex.

Daniel Defoe, *A Tour through the Whole Island of Great Britain, 1721–4*, edited by P. Rogers, 1971, pp. 165–6

The British economy was sufficiently advanced in the early eighteenth century to warrant the attention of European visitors. Henry Kalmeter was the first of the industrial spies who came to Scotland from Sweden in the course of the eighteenth century. Though employed by the Bergskollegium in Stockholm, the official body responsible for the Swedish mining industry, his diary is of value for more than this sector of the economy.

2.3   Travels in Scotland, 1719–20

In the lower parts or Shires of Scotland, although there is no want of mountains and hill where commonly is good feeding for sheep, yet the country is very fertile and gives a great deal of corn as well for fournishing the country as sometimes for exporting, especially to the Shire of Fife and Edinburgh, about Glasgow and Sterling, etc. where you can see the finest fields of barley, wheat, oats and peas, but rye is very little sown in that country. For feeding the ground they make use of limestone, which they spread over the ground mixed with dung or other rotten earth. In places near to the sea the[y] use for that purpose the dirt or seaweed that the sea throws up and is after that gathered of the people. And 'tho they reckon themselves pay'd when they get 4 corn after one, and in some places but 3, yet sometimes the ground yields 6, 8 and 10.

   The Highland again have but very little corn amongst theyr hills, but they are furnish'd and supply'd from the lower country, so they have fine feeding for cattle and sheeps, which are theyr greatest products . . . Although their cattle are smaller than the English yet, as they are sweeter and better flavoured, they are also in demand there, and so many are sent to England that the trade is thought to come to 40,000 pounds sterling a year.

Henry Kalmeter's Travels in Scotland, **edited by T.C. Smout, printed in** *Scottish Industrial History*, **Edinburgh, 1978, pp. 5–6, 14**

2.4   Advice to land stewards

A Steward should not forget to make the best enquiry into the disposition of any of the freeholders within or near any of his Lord's manors to sell their land, that he may use his best endeavours to purchase them at as reasonable a price, as may be for his Lord's advantage and convenience – especially in such manors, where improvements are to be made by inclosing commons and common-field; which (as every one, who is acquainted with the late improvement in agriculture, must know) is not a little advantageous to the nation in general as well as highly profitable to the undertaker. If the freeholders cannot all be persuaded to sell, yet at least an agreement for inclosing land should be pushed forward by the steward, and a scheme laid, wherein it may appear that an exact and proportional share will be allotted to every proprietor . . .

Edward Lawrence, *The Duty and Office of a Land Steward*, 3rd edition, 1731, p. 25

Questions

1 What evidence is there in these four sources for the diversity of agricultural experience in England and Scotland in the early eighteenth century?

2 How far did: (i) climate and soil; (ii) proximity to large towns; and (iii) the existence of 'improvements' account for this diversity?
3 Using source 2.2 show how far a 'rural economy' was more than simply farming.
4 The term 'improvement' has been used in the sources. What does it mean to Gough [2.1] and Lawrence [2.4]? Account for their contrasting views.
5 Historians have argued that awareness of markets was already evident by 1750. In what ways do these sources support this statement and what do they mean by 'market'?
6 'The British agricultural economy had already undergone a "revolution" in the early eighteenth century.' Discuss the validity of this statement.

Arthur Young: propagandist and journalist

Arthur Young (1741–1820) was born in London and educated in Suffolk. After failing to run a small farm successfully, he became an agricultural journalist, publishing over thirty books between 1767 and 1815 based on his extensive travels in Britain and on the Continent. His writings have received a mixed press from historians. Pat Rogers argues that as a populariser he 'describes the agricultural revolution of his times with intelligence as well as a great deal of brio. Occasionally we detect the glazed eye of the fanatic, but Young has too much common sense ever to be shrill' (Defoe, *A Tour through the Whole Island of Great Britain, 1721–4*, edited by P. Rogers, 1971, pp. 165–6). By contrast Chambers and Mingay maintain that he was 'the great apostle of improvement, and like all enthusiasts and propagandists he tended to overstate his case' (*The Agricultural Revolution 1750–1880*, 1966, p. 46).These views should be kept in mind when examining the sources below.

2.5   Young on cabbages

Cabbages, Mr Turner has cultivated from the year 1764, when he began his trials. That year he planted a rood and half, upon a piece of land that had been full of trees, which were stubbed. After this, it was ploughed in winter two or three times, and in the beginning of May planted in rows three feet asunder, the plants two feet from each other. They were only hand-hoed, but the operation was repeated three or four times: they were first used at Candlemas, for some fat oxen, and they ate them very heartily. They were Scotch cabbage. The experiment, though not conclusive, gave great hope of success on a larger scale.

A. Young, *A Six Months' Tour through the North of England*, 1770

2.6 Using clover

The second grand point of Mr Turner's husbandry, has been the introduction of clover. The farmers throughout Cleveland, have, to this day, rejected the use of this fine vegetable; notwithstanding their possessing a fine rich clay soil, which reason tells one, would produce vast crops of it. This gentleman has introduced the use of it with the same spirit he exerts in all his views. He has sown it upon large tracts of land and with great success.

Ibid.

2.7 Using grass

I [Sir Digby Legard of Ganton, Yorks] have enclosed 300 acres on the top of the wolds, and have laid down the greatest part with various kinds of grasses. Sainfoine makes the most general improvement, but it does not succeed in all parts alike, and indeed in some will not do at all; where the soil is shallowest and most gravelly, it prospers best. The greatest part of my sainfoine is drilled in rows a foot asunder, this takes but half the feed, and brings as good a crop as that which is sowed broadcast. White clover, rye-grasses, rib-grass and burnet, succeed pretty well with me, these grasses taken at an average, a good year with a bad one, and 30 or 40 acres together, yield near a ton of hay per acre, on land which never bore any hay before it was enclosed: I esteem this land to be now well worth 10s. an acre . . .

Ibid.

2.8 Improving moorland

Mr Thomas Elliot of Fremington is one of the greatest improvers of moorland in Yorkshire . . . His design was to enclose and improve a field every year; and this he accordingly has executed annually for several years. The method he takes to improve the black moorly land is this:

He pares and burns and limes it; and sows it with turnips; of which he gets a pretty good crop, worth on average about 40s. an acre. The next year he sows turnips again, and gets a second crop equally valuable as the first. After this he lays down to grass with rye grass, clover, hay-feeds etc., etc., He has tried some alone and with some oats; both do equally well, but the clover much the worse; the climate he apprehends much too cold for it; He often limes for every crop. The oats are frequently five quarters per acre. Potatoes he also cultivates . . . in rows two feet asunder and the sets one foot, and of these he gets often 100 bushels per acre . . . Some piece of this black land which he enclosed wanted drainage: and he has drained such effectually by drains two feet and an half wide at top; two feet and an half deep, and one foot wide at the bottom; the black earth thrown out he mixes with lime and finds it an excellent compost . . . This black land in its unimproved state, is worth to no tenant above 1s. 6d. an acre, but improved as above, would let very easily for 3s. . . .

Ibid.

2.9 Tradition and improvement

When I passed from the conversation of the farmers I was recommended to call on, to that of men whom chance threw in my way, I seemed to have lost a century of time, or to have moved a thousand miles in a day. Liberal communication, the result of enlarged ideas, was contrasted with a dark ignorance under the covert of wise suspicion; a sullen reserve lest landlords should be rendered too knowing; and false information given under the hope that it might deceive . . . The old open-field school must die off before new ideas can become generally rooted.

A. Young, *General View of the Agriculture of Oxfordshire*, 1809, pp. 35–6

Questions

1 What different methods for improving land do sources 2.5–2.8 identify? How successful were they in improving yields?
2 Why did landlords and farmers improve their land?
3 What evidence is there in these sources that improving land meant enclosing it?
4 Young contrasts attitudes to improved land with those to open fields in 2.9. How valid is this contrast?
5 How did farmers maintain or improve the fertility of their soil? Why were crops like clover so important to this process?
6 'Effective drainage was the key to the farming revolution on clay soils.' When, how and why?
7 In what ways do these sources demonstrate the strengths and weaknesses of Arthur Young as a propagandist for agrarian change?

According to Young, the emergence of new rotations, the development of selective breeding and greater landlord control over tenant farmers were pioneered by Lord Townshend, Robert Bakewell and Thomas Coke respectively. But turnips, an integral part of many new rotations, were already being grown when Townshend was still a child, the four course rotation, large farms and long leases existed before Coke was born and experiments with selective breeding were being carried out by forerunners of Bakewell in the early part of the century. So why did Young place such emphasis on their work?

2.10   Young on Townshend

Charles Lord Viscount Townshend . . . resigned the seals in May 1730; and, as he died in 1738, it is probable that this eight years was that of his improvements round Raynham . . . There is reason to believe that [he] actually introduced turnips in Norfolk; but the idea that he was the first who marled there is probably erroneous . . . But to be the father of the present great foundation of Norfolk husbandry, which had quadrupled the value of all the dry lands in the county, is an honour that merits the amplest eulogy. He certainly practised the turnip culture on such an extent, and with great success, that he was copied by all his neighbours . . .

A. Young, *Annals of Agriculture*, vol. V, 1786, pp. 120–4

2.11   Young on Bakewell

Mr Bakewell of Dishley [Leicestershire], one of the most considerable farmers in this country, has in so many instances improved on the husbandry of his neighbours, that he merits particular notice in this journal. His breed of cattle is famous throughout the kingdom; and he lately sent many to Ireland. He has in this part of his business many ideas which I believe are perfectly new; or have hitherto been totally neglected. This principle is to gain the best, whether sheep or cow, that will weigh most in the most valuable joints: there is a great difference between an ox of 50 stone carrying 30 in roasting pieces and 20 in coarse boiling – and another carrying 30 of the latter and 20 of the former . . . The general order in which Mr Bakewell keeps his cattle is pleasing; all are fat as bears; and this is a circumstance which he insists is owing to the excellence of the breed . . .

A. Young, *The Farmer's Tour through the East of England*, 1771, vol. I, pp. 110–113

2.12   Young on agriculture in Norfolk

Forty or fifty years ago, all the northern and western and part of the eastern tracts of the county, were sheep walks, let so low as from 6d. to 1s. 6d. and 2s. an acre. Much of it was in this condition only thirty years ago. The great improvements have been made by means of the following circumstances.
    First. By inclosing without the assistance of Parliament.
    Second. By a spirited use of marl and clay.
    Third. By the introduction of an excellent course of crops.
    Fourth. By the culture of turnips well hand-hoed.
    Fifth. By the culture of clover and rye grass.
    Sixth. By landlords granting long leases.
    Seventh. By the county being divided chiefly into large farms . . .
Great farms have been the soul of the Norfolk culture: split them into tenures of

an hundred pounds a year, you will find nothing but beggars and weeds in the whole county.

Ibid., vol. II, pp. 150, 156

Questions

1 What importance did Young ascribe to Townshend and Bakewell in documents **2.10** and **2.11**?
2 How convincing do you find Young's list of the reasons for the success of farming in Norfolk [**2.12**]? Explain your answer.
3 'People learn by example.' How far can this statement help to explain why Young focused on specific individuals when advocating improvement?
4 Using sources **2.5–2.11** assess Young's style as a writer. Who were his 'audience' and how effectively do you think he communicated with them?
5 Refer back to the quotations from Pat Rogers and Chambers and Mingay on page 29. Account for their different views.

A technological revolution

The 'revolution' in eighteenth-century farming was a combination of enclosure, the more widespread application of existing methods of production and the use of iron tools and more efficient tools (a move, for example, from using the sickle to the scythe). However, the contribution of the eighteenth-century pioneers has proved less real than that supposed by Young and his contemporaries. It was then followed in the first half of the nineteenth century by a 'technological revolution' with the application of labour-saving machinery, drainage and artificial fertilisers.

2.13 James Caird on continued diversity

To show the progress which has been made in the art of agriculture in this country, it is not necessary to go back to any authority of the last century for a description of the processes then adopted. Every county presents contrasts abundantly instructive, the most antiquated and the most modern systems being found side by side. The successful practices of one far, or one county, are unknown or unheeded in the next.

James Caird, *English Agriculture in 1850–51*, 1852, p. 498

2.14   A French view of English farming in 1860: Hippolyte Taine

No central farmyard: the farm is a collection of fifteen or twenty low buildings, in brick, economically designed and built . . . Bullocks, pigs, sheep, each in a well-aired, well-cleaned stall. We were shown a system of byres in which the floor is a grating . . . Steam engines for all the work of the arable land. A narrow-gauge railway to carry their food to the animals; they eat chopped turnips, crushed beans and 'oil cakes'. Farming in these terms is a complicated industry based on theory and experiment, constantly being perfected and equipped with cleverly designed tools.

Taine's Notes on England, p. 132, quoted in Chambers and Mingay, *The Agricultural Revolution 1750–1880*, 1966, pp. 173–4

Questions

1 How had 'new technology' made farming 'a complicated industry'?
2 Compare source 2.13 with 2.9. In what ways do they suggest reasons why change in agriculture was uneven? Why do you think this was the case?
3 'Technological advances in the nineteenth century resolved many of the unsolved problems of eighteenth-century farming.' Discuss.
4 By 1850 British farming was a combination of 'old' and 'new'. In what ways does this cast doubt on the validity of the notion of an 'agricultural revolution'?

Enclosure and agricultural change

The most dramatic expression of change in farming came with widespread parliamentary enclosure from the mid eighteenth century. In those areas enclosed the large open and common fields and wastes were replaced by the chequerboard pattern of smaller fields with new roads, bridges and buildings. Enclosure had important consequences for agricultural workers. New technology and falling profits on arable land from the mid 1810s to the mid 1830s led to falling wages and efforts by farmers to reduce labour costs further. These issues can be explored in more detail in Richard Brown, *Change and Continuity in British Society 1800–1850*, 1987, pp. 38–47. This section will focus on the economic arguments for and against enclosing land.

2.15a   The commons before enclosure

It was mostly fine, green sward or pasturage, broken or divided, indeed, with clumps of blossom'd whins, foxgloves, fern and some juniper, and with heather in profusion, sufficient to scent the whole air . . . On this common – the poor man's heritage for ages past, where he kept a few sheep or a Kyloe cow, perhaps a flock of geese, mostly a stock of bee-hives – it was infinite pleasure that I lay and beheld the beautiful wild scenery . . .

Thomas Bewick, *A Memoir of Thomas Bewick, Written by Himself*, 1862, London, 1961, p. 27. He wrote the book in the 1820s.

2.15b   William Marshall takes a contrary view

Upon the waste commons of the West Riding the kind of sheep bred are more miserable than can be imagined. They generally belong to poor people and are in small lots so that they can never be improved. This will apply to the whole of the sheep on the common that are not stinted; the numbers put on beggar and starve the lot.

William Marshall, *The Rural Economy of Yorkshire*, 2 vols., 1788

2.15c   Advantages of enclosing the commons

Inclosing – The benefits and advantages that would be derived from a general inclosure of commons, are so numerous as far to exceed my powers of description or computation. The opportunity it would afford, of separating dry ground from wet, of well draining the latter, and liming the rotten parts, is of infinite consequence; as such an arrangement would, with the aid of intelligent breeders, by the means of raising a breed of sheep and neat cattle far superior to the present race of wretched half-starved animals now seen in such situations . . . Furthermore the livestock would, by this means, be rendered many hundreds per cent more valuable to individuals and the community, than it has hitherto been, or can possibly be, without enclosure . . . It does not appear to be necessary to state with precision, nor indeed is it capable of being so stated, what would be the increase in value of the commons of this country on their being enclosed and well and properly cultivated. It may, however, with safety be stated at upwards of 15 times their present value to the proprietors, and 40 times their present value to the public.

John Middleton, *A View of the Agriculture of Middlesex*, 1789

Questions

1 Bewick was an engraver of birds. How do you think this influenced his view of the common fields?
2 What are the main arguments employed by Marshall and Middleton in justifying the enclosure of land?

3 Enclosure resulted in the replacement of communal by individual rights. What were the economic benefits of this process to: (i) the landowners; and (ii) the tenant farmers?

4 'The role of enclosure in the rationalising of land usage between 1750 and 1850 has been exaggerated.' Examine the validity of this statement.

2.16a   An official justification of enclosure

Let us begin with taking a view of the objections which have been stated to this species of improvement, and see if we cannot prove them to be for the most part either false or frivolous.

1st. Invasion of the rights and interests of the cottagers. The foremost of these objections carries with it the appearance of a humane attention to the comfort of the poor; but a brief investigation will lessen its influence, if not totally refute it.

There are but two modes of enclosing commons. First, by unanimous consent of the parties claiming rights, who delegate power to commissioners, chosen by themselves, to ascertain their validity, and divide them accordingly under covenants and agreements properly drawn and executed for the purpose. Or secondly, by Act of Parliament obtained by the petition of a certain proportion of the commoners, both in number and value, whereby a minority, sanctioned only by ignorance, prejudice or selfishness, is precluded from defeating the ends of private advantage and public utility.

In point of economy, the first of these methods is most eligible . . . But it is seldom practised unless in commons on a small scale from the difficulty of procuring the consent of every individual claimant, without which it cannot be accomplished.

In either of these methods, it is manifest that the right of the cottager cannot be invaded; since with respect to legal and equitable construction, he stands precisely on the same ground with his more opulent neighbour; and as to his interest, I can truly declare that, in all the cases which have fallen within my observation, enclosures have meliorated his condition, by exciting a spirit of activity and industry, whereby habits of sloth have been by degrees overcome, and supineness and inactivity have been exchanged for vigour and exertion.

Survey of the Board of Agriculture for Somersetshire, 1798

2.16b   A contrasting view

The general objections to the inclosure of fields are, that it tends to diminish the growth of corn, throws the lands when thus parcelled out into fewer hands, and renders a lesser quality of labour necessary to the management of them. Circumstances these which, it is urged, invariably tend to depopulation and wretchedness.

It is urged against the inclosure of commons, etc., that the quantity of pasturages is diminished by this practice . . . and that the heath and waste lands being in general stocked with young cattle, the inclosure of these strikes at the very root of their plenty. And it is further objected, in many instances, that the poor cottagers, who have a right of commoning, are hereby deprived of a kind of property which long possession has endeared to them, which is in fact extremely conducive to their subsistence and in some degree also beneficial to the public . . .

The objections, however, made to the first kind of inclosure would be undoubtedly of great weight supposing none but tillage land be inclosed. Though the produce of some kind or other would perhaps be increased upon the whole, and the net produce very considerably, it would remain matter of some doubt whether the advantages would in a public view counterbalance the great evils of depopulation and decrease in labour. But in a country full of trade and manufactures this evil is perhaps more in appearance than reality. The hands spared by these improvements are not thrown upon the public, but may be employed in a manner equally beneficial to it and themselves . . .

Nathaniel Forster, *An Enquiry into the Cause of the Present High Price of Provisions*, 1767, pp. 117–21

Questions

1 In **2.16a** what different ways of enclosing land are outlined?
2 What advantages can be found in **2.16a** in favour of enclosing land?
3 Forster identifies several disadvantages of enclosure. How does he deal with these objections?
4 In what ways do both sources overestimate the economic security of cottagers?
5 'Economic advantage is often bought with human misery.' Consider this statement in relation to agricultural change between 1750 and 1850.

Increasing output

The extent to which there was an increase in agricultural output in England and Wales can be ascertained by comparing estimates made by Arthur Young in 1770 and J.R. McCulloch in 1846 (see Tables 2.17a–b over).

2.17a   Table showing output in 1770

	A. Arable		
	Acreage (m. acres)	*Yield (bushels p.a.)*	*Value (£m)*
Wheat	2.8	24	16.770
Barley	2.6	32	10.496
Oats	1.5	38	5.636
Beans and peas	0.9	B.33 P.23	4.060
Turnips	1.7	£2.25 p.a.	3.629
Clover	3.2	£5.40 p.a.	16.647
Fallow and other crops	0.8		
TOTAL	13.5		£57,237,759

	B. Animal Husbandry		
	Numbers	*Produce per head*	*Value (£m)*
Cows	741,532	£5.10s.	4.078
Sheep	22,188,948	11s.8d.	12.944
Fatting cattle	513,369	£5	2.567
Young cattle	912,656	£1	0.913
Swine	1,711,200	15s.	1.283
Poultry			0.171
TOTAL			£21,955,988
GRAND TOTAL			£79,193,747

In addition Young estimated that there were 684,491 horses employed on farms in England and Wales.

From A. Young, *The Farmer's Tour through the East of England,* 1770, vol. IV, pp. 256–61

2.17b   Table showing output in 1846

	A. Arable		
	Acreage (m.)	Yield (bushels p.a.)	Value (£)
Wheat	3.8	32	32,571,427
Barley	1.5	34	8,196,429
Oats/rye	2.5	40	10,714,429
Beans/peas	1.5	30	2,410,714
Potatoes, rape and turnips	2.0	valued at	23,100,000
Clover	1.3	£7 p.a.	
Fallow	1.5		
Hops	0.05	£15 p.a.	750,000
Gardens	0.15	£15 p.a.	2,250,000
TOTAL	14.30		£79,992,999

	B. Animal Husbandry	
Cattle	1,200,000 at £12 each	14,400,000
Calves	200,000 at £3 each	600,000
Sheep and lambs	6,800,000 at £1.10s each	10,200,000
Wool	360,000 packs at £12 each (excluding slaughtered sheep)	4,320,000
Hog and pig	550,000 at £1.16s each	1,000,000
Horses	200,000 full grown at £15 each	3,000,000
Poultry, eggs, rabbits, etc.		1,344,000
Meadow and grass for work and pleasure horses		13,000,000
Dairy produce		12,000,000
Wood		1,750,000
TOTAL		61,614,000
GRAND TOTAL		£141,606,999

From J.R. McCulloch, *Statistical Account*, 1847, pp. 549–50

Questions

1 Young admitted frankly that the evidence he collected in his three tours did not cover the whole country. In what ways does this call into question the validity of **2.17a**?

2 In what ways does a comparison between **2.17a** and **2.17b** show the effects of agricultural change?

3 'Agricultural output was increased by the more effective use of existing resources.' How far do these sources support this statement?

4 In what ways was farming more profitable in 1846 than in 1770?

5 'Statistics often tell historians more about statisticians than economic trends.' Discuss this in relation to agricultural change.

6 Using sources **2.1–2.17b** construct a chronology of agricultural change 1750–1850. What problems does your chronology pose for historians?

Landscape, art and literature

The final section of this chapter examines how changes in farming and in the rural landscape were reflected in contemporary art and literature. How far were the perceptions of writers and painters 'romantic' ones or did they have a 'realistic' view of the rural experience?

2.18 John Constable: *The Haywain*, 1821

2.19 Samuel Palmer: *A Rustic Scene*, 1825

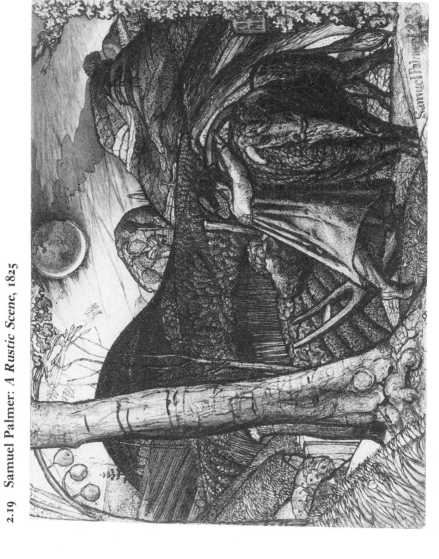

2.20 W.H. Pyne: *Country Work*. From *Microcosm: or, a picturesque delineation of the Arts, Agriculture, Manufactures, etc. of Great Britain*, 1808

Ploughing

Harvest

Harvest

Reproduced by courtesy of **The Mansell Collection**

2.21   William Holman Hunt: *The Hireling Shepherd*, 1851

Questions

1 In what ways do these painters give a stylised view of the rural landscape? How does their work reflect change in the countryside?
2 The view of life in the countryside that these artists give is one of rustic simplicity. Why was this?
3 'British artists between 1750 and 1850 made little social comment in their representation of rural Britain'. Discuss.

2.22   A eulogy for rustic England?

Many poets and essayists have eulogised rustic life and manners, as being replete with sylvan joys, arcadian scenes, primeval innocence and unsophisticated pleasures. Alas! these are but the closet dreams of metropolitan poets and visionary enthusiasts; for I fear that all their pleasing pictures are wholly drawn from imagination, and not from nature.

The Autobiography of John Britton, part I, 1850, p. 59

Questions

1 In what ways does John Britton's statement help in understanding the value of: (i) art; and (ii) literature as historical sources?
2 'Art and literature can provide historical knowledge and even be forms of history.' Discuss in relation to the sources in this chapter.
3 'A landscape in art or literature is a view, not only of the countryside, but also of the moral and social attitudes of the artists and writers and their audience.' In what ways is this reflected in the sources?

The use of the changing landscape to reflect changes in moral character can be examined in the literature of the period. In the mid eighteenth-century novel the landed estate was seen as a social and moral ideal, an expression of stability. However, the impact of enclosure, the intensification of rural poverty and the social upheavals occasioned by revolution abroad and urbanisation at home led to the development of themes of disturbance and nostalgia in both novels and poetry.

2.23   Jane Austen

He had been visiting a friend in a neighbouring county, and that friend having recently had his grounds laid out by an improver, Mr Rushworth was returned with his head full of the subject and very eager to be improving his own place in the same way; and though not saying much to the purpose, could talk of nothing else. The subject has been already handled in the drawing-room; it was revived in the dining-parlour. Mis Bertram's attention and opinion was evidently his chief aim; and though her deportment showed rather conscious superiority than any solicitude to oblige him, the mention of Sotherton Court, and the ideas attached to it, gave her a feeling of complacency, which prevented her from being ungracious.

'I wish you could see Compton,' he said, 'it is the most complete thing! I never saw a place so altered in my life . . . I declare when I got back to Sotherton yesterday, it looked like a prison – quite a dismal, old prison.'

'Oh! for shame!' cried Mrs Norris. 'A prison, indeed! Sotherton Court is the noblest old place in the world.'

'It wants improvement, ma'am, beyond any thing. I never saw a place that wanted so much improvement in my life; and it is so forlorn, that I do not know what can be done with it.'

Jane Austen, *Mansfield Park*, 1814, Penguin edition, 1966, pp. 84–5

2.24   Anthony Trollope

Its green pastures, its waving wheat, its deep and shady and – let us add – dirty lanes, its paths and stiles, its tawny-coloured, well-built rural churches, its avenues of beeches and frequent Tudor mansions, its constant county hunt, its social graces, and the air of clanship which pervades it, has made it to its own inhabitants a favoured land of Goshen. It is purely agricultural: agricultural in its produce, agricultural in its poor, and agricultural in its pleasures . . . England is not yet a commercial country in the sense in which that epithet is used for her; and let us hope that she will not soon become so. She might surely as well be called feudal England, or chivalrous England. If in western civilised Europe there does exist a nation among whom there are high signors, and with whom the owners of land are the true aristocracy, the aristocracy that is trusted as being best and fitted to rule, that nation is the English.

A. Trollope, *Doctor Thorne*, 1858, quoted in R. Williams, *The Country and the City*, 1975, pp. 213–14

Questions

1 In what ways do these sources make agricultural change a 'moral' issue?
2 How convincing do you find Trollope's argument that 'England is not yet a commercial country . . .' and why?
3 'The polarity in rural England between tradition and change is a literary construct which has little to do with history.' Discuss.

4 'Literature is a reflection of existing social and moral values. It does not create them.' How far do these sources support this view and in what ways?

Richard Cobden spoke of the growth of railways as ending the feudalism of the countryside in the mid nineteenth century. But at the same time Feargus O'Connor was attempting to establish his Land Plan. A belief in 'this green and pleasant land', a nostalgic yearning for rustic simplicity and rural charms and a desire to get 'back to the land' are still powerful images. Grounded in a mythic view of the past, they neglect the reality of agriculture in the eighteenth and nineteenth centuries, placing an emphasis on the social losses rather than the economic gains of change. Agriculture retained its importance in the 1850s for its contribution to the total economy but also in its 'moral' certitude. Landscape could conjure up images of tradition which 'improvement' could not alter.

3 Technological change and the organisation of industry

In his *Lives of the Engineers* Samuel Smiles, the mid-Victorian apostle of self-help, wrote that:

Our engineers may be regarded as the makers of modern civilization . . . Are not the men who have made the motive power of the country, and immensely increased its productive strength, the men above all others who have tended to make this country what it is?

By contrast W.W. Rostow wrote in 1975 in *How It All Began: Origins of the Modern Economy* that:

Invention and innovation at any period of time are marginal activities in society . . . Life goes on in familiar ways, with familiar technologies, while the creative few dream their dreams and struggle. Only looking backwards . . . are the achievements of the inventors and innovators generally understood, appreciated and accorded a grand place in history.

The technological and scientific achievements between 1700 and 1850 were substantial. The immense force of that achievement has conventionally been examined in relation to the great inventors and inventions. However, as Rostow indicated, new technologies were not always recognised by contemporaries as 'revolutionary' or advantageous to productive capacity. Machinery was an issue that was contested and resisted. Understanding change in textile production, iron making and coal output, all areas in which 'new' technology played a major role, is not as simple as historians once believed. This chapter will consider the 'revolutionary' nature of technology and why it became an issue after 1800 in three respects. First, the 'machinery question' will be examined. This will be followed by a consideration of the impact of what many contemporaries and later historians have seen as *the* symbol of the 'industrial revolution' – steam power. Finally, the nature of 'proto-industrialisation' and the extent and character of larger units of production will be discussed.

The machinery question

In the eighteenth century the machine was seen as contributing to the general 'improvement' of society and was viewed with a sense of excitement. In the aftermath of the French wars the prospect of a harmonious integration of social and economic progress was called into question. Machines were often unfairly blamed for crises in the economy and for the growing sense of social division in the rapidly expanding cotton towns. Belief in economic progress was for some contemporaries replaced by resentment, opposition and fear at what was perceived as the 'dehumanisation' of labour in the face of technological advance. Machinery became an issue.

3.1 Thomas Carlyle and 'An Age of Machinery'

The huge demon of Mechanism smokes and thunders, panting at his great task, in all sections of English land; changing his shape like a very Proteus; and infallibly at every change of change, oversetting whole multitudes of workmen, as if with the waving of his shadow from afar, hurling them asunder, this way and that, in their crowded march and curse of work or traffic.

Thomas Carlyle, 'Chartism', *Critical and Miscellaneous Essays, Collected Works*, vol. XXIII, 1839, p. 24

Were we required to characterise this age of ours by any single epithet, we should be tempted to call it, not an Heroical, Devotional, Philosophical, or Moral Age, but above all others, the Mechanical Age. It is the Age of Machinery, in every outward and inward sense of that word; the age which, with its whole undivided might, forwards, teaches and practises, the great art of adapting means to ends. Nothing is now done directly, or by hand . . . Our old modes of exertion are all discredited and thrown aside. On every hand, the living artisan is driven from his workshop, to make room for the speedier, inanimate one. The shuttle drops from the fingers of the weaver, and falls into iron fingers that ply it faster . . . Everything has its cunningly devised implements, its pre-established apparatus, it is not done by hand, but by machinery.

Thomas Carlyle, 'Signs of the Times', 1829, printed in A. Shelston (ed.), *Thomas Carlyle: Selected Writings*, 1971, pp. 64-5

Questions

1 What does Carlyle mean by an 'Age of Machinery'? In what ways does he contrast it with earlier 'ages'?
2 What literary devices does Carlyle use to convey his views of machinery in the two passages?

3 It is not the economic benefits but the social effects that Carlyle emphasised. Why do you think he did this?
4 The two passages were published ten years apart. How far had Carlyle changed his views and why?
5 'Carlyle's social criticism was virtually inseparable from his propaganda.' Do you agree? Explain your answer fully.

3.2   Robert Owen

The introduction of the steam engine and the spinning machine added in an extraordinary manner to the powers of human nature. In their consequences they have in half a century multiplied the productive power, or the means of creating wealth, among the population of these islands, more than twelve-fold, besides giving a great increase to the means of creating wealth in other countries.

The steam engine and spinning machines, with the endlesss mechanical inventions to which they have given rise, have, however, inflicted evils on society, which now greatly over-balance the benefits which are derived from them. They have created an aggregate of wealth, and placed it in the hands of a few, who, by its aid, continue to absorb the wealth produced by the industry of the many. Thus the mass of the population are become mere slaves to the ignorance and caprice of these monopolists, and are far more truly helpless and wretched than they were before the names of WATT and ARKWRIGHT were known. Yet these celebrated and ingenious men have been the instruments of preparing society for the important beneficial changes which are about to occur.

All now know that the good which these inventions are calculated to impart to the community have not yet been realised. The condition of society, instead of being improved, has been deteriorated, under the new circumstances to which they have given birth; and it is now experiencing a retrograde movement.

'Something,' therefore 'must be done,' as the general voice exclaims, to give to our suffering population, and to society at large, the means of deriving from these inventions the advantages which all men of science expect from them.

Robert Owen, 'Report to the County of Lanark', 1820, printed in Robert Owen, *A New View of Society and Other Writings*, 1972, p. 258

Questions

1 What were Robert Owen's basic criticisms of machinery?
2 Owen believed in cooperation. How far does this explain his attitude to machinery and why?
3 Owen's critique of machinery was a moral one. Do you find this convincing and why?

The incidence of slump, as in 1826 and in 1830, was blamed on machinery. Machines were tangible and could consequently be destroyed while other things which were more responsible for economic stability like demand or capital investment could not.

3.3   Simonde de Sismondi in 1826

This permanent and universal glut is absolutely inexplicable on the system of your economists Messrs. Ricardo, McCulloch etc., but it is in my opinion a necessary consequence of the direction industry has taken . . . I have never dreamt of preventing by any law the improvement of machinery, not even of discouraging ingenious men from the invention of new machines; all that I should wish is to render it impossible for the master manufacturers to extort from their workmen what they cannot obtain from the consumer.

J.C.L. Simonde de Sismondi to Edward Baines jun., 27 July 1826, quoted in M. Berg, *The Machinery Question and the Making of Political Economy 1815–1848*, Cambridge, 1980, p. 104

3.4   Nassau Senior in 1830

Have not even magistrates and landlords recommended the destruction, or, what is the same, both in principle and effect, the disuse of every machine of which the object is to render labour more efficient in the production of articles consumed by the labourer in the production of that very fund on the extent of which, compared with the number to be maintained, the amount of wages depend? . . . Threshing machines are the present objects of hostility, ploughs will be next.

N.W. Senior, *Three Lectures on the Rate of Wages*, London, 1831, p. iii

3.5   Engels

Every improvement in machinery leads to unemployment, and the greater the technical improvement the greater the unemployment . . . The middle classes coolly ignore the fact that it takes years before the decline in prices of the manufactured goods leads to the opening of new factories. Moreover, the middle classes fail to mention the fact that every technical innovation shifts more and more of the physical labour from the worker to the machine. Consequently, tasks once performed by grown men are no longer necessary . . . The division of labour has intensified the brutalising effects of forced labour. In most branches of industry the task of the worker is limited to insignificant and purely repetitive tasks which continue minute by minute for every day of the year . . . The introduction of steam power, and machinery has had the same result. The physical labour of the worker has been lightened, he is spared some of his former exertion, but the task itself is trifling and extremely monotonous.

Friedrich Engels, *The Condition of the Working Class in England*, 1845, edited by W.O. Henderson and W.H. Chaloner, Oxford, 1958, pp. 151, 153, 134

Questions

1 Using sources 3.3–3.5 examine how far economic distress in the early nineteenth century can be explained by the development of technology.
2 Nassau Senior [3.4] said that magistrates and landowners suggested the destruction of machinery. Why should they have suggested this?
3 Why did demands for an ending of technological advance occur during periods of economic slump?
4 What arguments does Engels [3.5] put forward to support his case against machinery? How convincing do you find them?
5 Compare Carlyle [3.1] and Engels [3.5] as social critics. What techniques of persuasion do they use?
6 'The debate on the machinery question was as much a political as an economic one.' Discuss this statement.

Attitudes to machinery were diverse. For many Tories opposition to technology was part of their protest against the suppression of rural society it knew by an industrial society it knew not. Workers criticised the rapid and unplanned introduction of new techniques when it led to technological unemployment. But radical leaders took up contradictory positions. For some machines were fundamental to their utopian dreams, but many more saw them as the cause of economic distress. Challenged from both sides the middle classes had to find explanations for the social and economic impact of the machine. For them political economy, with its philosophy of the free market, provided an ideological solution.

3.6   David Ricardo

The natural price of all commodities, excepting raw produce and labour, has a tendency to fall, in the progress of wealth and population; for though, on the one hand, they are enhanced in real value, from the rise in the natural price of the raw material of which they are made, this is more than counter-balanced by the improvements in machinery, by the better division and distribution of labour, and by the increasing skill, both in science and art, of the producers.

David Ricardo, *Principles of Political Economy and Taxation*, 1817, edited by Donald Winch, 1971, pp. 115–16

3.7   John Stuart Mill

The labour of Watt in contriving the steam engine was as essential a part of production as that of the mechanics who build or the engineers who work the instrument . . . In the national, or universal point of view the labour of the savant, or speculative thinker, is as much a part of production in the very narrowest sense, as that of the inventor of a practical art; many such inventions having been the direct consequence of theoretic discoveries, and every extension of knowledge of the powers of nature being fruitful of applications to the purposes of outward life.

J.S. Mill, *Principles of Political Economy*, London, 1848, p. 42

Questions

1 In what ways do Ricardo and Mill present a common defence of machinery and in what ways do their views differ?
2 Mill emphasised the link between the 'savant' and the 'inventor of a practical art'. What did he mean by this?
3 Why did political economy become the economic ideology of the middle classes?
4 'The debate on machinery was no debate at all. Conservatives emphasised social issues, radicals political effects and the middle class an economic justification.' Discuss this statement.

The steam engine: symbol of industrialisation

The association between the adoption of steam power and the rise of modern industry has been a familiar theme since the early nineteenth century. Contemporaries applauded the inventions of James Watt as the greatest the world had seen. The key position of the steam engine was reaffirmed by subsequent economic historians. Arnold Toynbee, who popularised the notion of the 'industrial revolution' in the 1880s, saw it as the lynchpin of invention: mechanisation would have been retarded without the existence of the prime-mover. T.S. Ashton (1948) emphasised that 'The new forms of power . . . were the pivot on which industry swung into the modern age', while David Landes in *The Unbound Prometheus* (1969) says that 'the introduction of engines for converting heat into work, thereby opened to man a new and almost unlimited supply of energy'. But just how pivotal was the steam engine?

3.8   Contemporary praise

The great motive power which the genius of Watt had first disciplined . . . was applied, about the year 1785 in furtherance of the discoveries of Arkwright, and the combination of the steam engine with the spinning frame, [not only] changed an aspect of production [but also] gave rise to a new class of problems, bearing upon the distribution of the produce.

Travers Twiss, *View of the Progress of Political Economy in Europe, since the Sixteenth Century*, London, 1847, pp. 226–7

3.9   The inhumanity of steam

A special contrast, as every man was in the forest of looms where Stephen worked, to the crashing, smashing, tearing piece of mechanism at which he laboured. Never fear, good people of an anxious turn of mind, that Art will consign Nature to oblivion. Set anywhere, side by side, the work of GOD and the work of men; and the former, even though it be a troop of Hands of very small account, will gain in dignity from this comparison.

So many hundred Hands in this Mill; so many hundred horse Steam Power. It is known, to the force of a single pound weight what the engine will do; but, not all the calculations of the National Debt can tell me the capacity for good or evil, for love or hatred, for patriotism or discontent, for the decomposition of virtue into vice, or the reverse, at any single moment in the soul of one of these its quiet servants, with the composed faces and the regulated actions. There is no mystery in it; there is an unfathomable mystery in the meanest of them, for ever – Supposing we were to reserve our arithmetic for material objects, and to govern these awful unknown quantities by other means!

Charles Dickens, *Hard Times*, 1854, edited by D. Craig, 1970, pp. 107–8

Questions

1 Dickens and Twiss give contrasting views of the steam engine. How do you account for this contrast?
2 Twiss recognised 'the genius of Watt' but did not acknowledge the role of Thomas Newcomen in developing steam power. Why do you think this was the case?
3 'Steam power + new machines = an industrial revolution.' Discuss this statement in relation to Twiss and Dickens.

4 How far did steam power lead to new methods of production up to the
mid nineteenth century?

3.10   Marx on machines

John Stuart Mill says in his *Principles of Political Economy*: 'It is questionable if
all the mechanical inventions yet made have lightened the day's toil of any human
being.' That is, however, by no means the aim of the application of machinery
under capitalism. Like every other instrument for increasing the productivity of
labour, machinery is intended to cheapen commodities and, by shortening the
part of the working day in which the worker works for himself, to lengthen the
other part, the part he gives to the capitalist for nothing. . . . The steam engine
itself, such as it was at its invention during the manufacturing period at the close
of the seventeenth century, and such as it continued to be down to 1780, did not
give rise to any industrial revolution. It was, on the contrary, the invention of
machines that made a revolution in the form of the steam engines necessary. As
soon as man, instead of working on the object of labour with a tool, becomes
merely the motive power of a machine, it is purely accidental that the motive
power happens to be clothed in the form of human muscles; wind, water or steam
could just as well take man's place . . .

K. Marx, *Capital*, vol. 1, Pelican edition, 1976, pp. 492, 496–7

3.11   John Morton on costs

In January 1861, John C. Morton read before the Society of Arts a paper on 'The
Forces Employed in Agriculture'. He states there: 'Every improvement that
furthers the uniformity of the land makes the steam engine more and more
applicable to the production of pure mechanical force . . . Horse-power is needed
wherever crooked fences and other obstructions prevent uniform action. These
obstructions are vanishing day by day. For operations that demand more exercise
of will than actual force, the only power applicable is that controlled every instant
by the human mind – in other words, man-power.' Mr Morton then reduces
steam-power, horse-power and man-power to the unit in general use for the steam
engine . . . and reckons the cost of one horse-power from a steam engine to be
3d. per hour and from a horse 5.5d. . . .

Ibid., footnote, pp. 497–8

3.12   Barlow on costs

Now the value of 80 lbs, or about a bushel of coals [for the engines], we can
scarcely estimate at more than 1s., the expense of 1.5 horse-keep will perhaps be,
at a medium about 3s.6d., while the expense of 7.5 men, at the medium rate of
wages for good English labourers will be 21s. This, however, is not a fair view of
the subject, because in the latter case the whole expense is included, whereas in

the horse we must consider the first purchase, the expense of harness, stabling, shoeing, grooming, &.; this perhaps may raise the daily expense of the horse to 4s.6d.; and in steam-power we have also, besides the expense of the fuel, to include that of oil, tallow, the engineer, stoker, the first purchase, erection of building; and this will probably in a medium-sized engine, amount to another shilling per day.

P. Barlow, 'A Treatise on the Manufactures and Machinery of Great Britain', *Encyclopaedia Metropolitana*, vol. VI: *Mixed Sciences*, London, 1836, p. 91

3.13   Criticism of steam power: John Smeaton, 1781

Secondly, all the fire engines that I have seen are liable to stoppages, and that so suddenly, that in making a single stroke the machine is capable of passing from almost full power and motion to a total cessation . . . By the intervention of water, these uncertainties and difficulties are avoided, for the work, in fact, is a water-mill . . .

Quoted in R.L. Hills, *Power in the Industrial Revolution*, Manchester, 1970, p. 136

3.14   Criticism of steam power: Thomas Wicksteed, 1840

The irregularity of the action of the steam in ordinary low-pressure engines is very nearly counterbalanced by the use of a fly-wheel; nevertheless, in some of the cotton factories, (for instance, that is Messrs. Lane, of Stockport) two engines are employed to work the same machinery, the cranks being fixed at right angles to each other, as in marine engines. This arrangement equalizes the action of the steam still more, yet the motion is not so regular as that of an overshot water wheel, where the supply of water is uniform, as it would be in this case . . .

Thomas Wicksteed, *Civil Engineer and Architect's Journal*, no. 3, 1840, quoted in G.N. Von Tunzelmann, *Steam Power and British Industrialization to 1860*, Oxford, 1978, pp. 142–3

3.15   Grenville Withers questioned

Q: Do you find generally throughout Belgium that English steam engines are getting into disrepute? *A*: They are getting into very great disrepute, in general, because they consume so much coal; English manufacturers having coal extremely cheap, pay very little attention to how much the engine consumes . . . we calculate, in England, that a low-pressure engine will burn about 10 lbs per horse-power per hour, whereas the manufacturers abroad pretend that Wolf's engine burns something under 8, and they go down to 6.

Evidence before the Select Committee on the Exportation of Machinery, 1841, *Parliamentary Papers*, 1841, vol. VII, questions 640–1

3.16   Table showing horse-power used in textile factories

		1838	*1850*	*1856*
Cotton	Water	12,977	11,550	9,131
	Steam	46,826	71,005	88,001
Woollen and worsted	Water	10,405	10,314	9,842
	Steam	17,389	23,345	30,963
Flax, jute and hemp	Water	3,678	3,387	3,935
	Steam	7,412	10,905	14,387
Silk	Water	928	853	816
	Steam	2,457	2,858	4,360

A.E. Musson, *The Growth of British Industry*, 1978, p. 112

Questions

1 Explain Marx's view of machinery and its costs in documents 3.10 and 3.11. How convincing do you find his views?
2 Compare the analysis of the costs of power in 3.11 and 3.12.
3 What criticisms of steam power can be found in documents 3.13–3.15? Why do you think British manufacturers were wasteful in their use of energy?
4 Using document 3.16 examine the proposition that the 'industrial revolution' was not simply based on steam power.
5 'It was the application of high- *not* low-pressure steam power which revolutionised the British economy.' Discuss.
6 Have historians stressed the impact of steam power too much?

From proto-industry to factories

How can historians explain the change that occurred between the late eighteenth and mid nineteenth centuries in the organisation of manufacturing production? Industrialisation was dominated by increased specialisation, division of labour, innovation, skill and mechanisation. Historians now look to the emergence of cottage industries rather than urban workshops for the crucial transitional phase of economic development. This stage is now popularly called 'proto-industrialisation'. Between the seventeenth and nineteenth centuries there was a great increase in manufacturing production in the countryside. Rural industry was frequently domestic, often being combined with farming. It supplied regional, national and international markets. Proto-industry is credited not simply with sources of labour and capital but with the entrepreneurship and technical and organisational changes that led to the first major increases in productivity before the factory. It is, however, important to recognise the existence and importance of the urban artisan and that, as late as 1851, the majority of people employed in Britain still worked in the unmechanised sectors. Cottage industries did not disappear with the development of factories, even in those branches of production most affected by this innovation of new technology.

3.17   Defoe on the Yorkshire woollen industry

Then it was I began to perceive the reason and nature of the thing, and found that this division of land into small pieces and scattering of the dwellings, was occasioned by, and done for the convenience of the business which the people were generally employ'd in, and that, as I said before, though we saw no people stirring without doors, yet they are full within . . . Among the manufacturers' houses are likewise scattered an infinite number of cottages or small dwellings, in which dwell the workmen which are employed, the women and children of whom, are always busy carding, spinning, etc. so that no hands being unemploy'd, all can gain their bread, even from the youngest to the ancient; hardly any thing above four years old, but its hands are sufficient to it self . . . if we knock'd at the door of any of the master manufacturers, we presently saw a house full of lusty fellows, some at the dye-fat, some dressing the cloths, some in the loom, some one thing, some another, all hard at work, and full employed upon the manufacture, and all seeming to have sufficient business . . .

Daniel Defoe, *A Tour through the Whole Island of Great Britain*, 1724–6, Penguin edition, 1971, pp. 491–3

3.18   Arthur Young on the Norwich worsted industry

The staple manufacturers are crapes and camblets; besides which they make in great abundance damasks, sattins, alopeens . . . They work up the Leicestershire and Lincolnshire wool chiefly, which is brought here for combing and spinning, while the Norfolk wool goes to Yorkshire for carding and cloths . . . The earnings of the manufacturers are various but in general high . . . In respect to the present state of the manufacture, it is neither brisk, nor very dull. They could execute more orders than they have; and some among them complain because they have not so great a trade as during the war; for then they could not answer the demand, for it was so uncommonly great (from 1743 to 1763 was their famous aera). This was however owing in some measure to many manufacturers exporting so largely on speculation, that the markets have been overstocked since . . .

Arthur Young, *The Farmer's Tour through the East of England*, 1771, vol. II, pp. 74–7

3.19 Trade in decline

The Norwich trade has for some years been in a declining state, which is ascribed to the following causes: to the prevalent taste for wearing cottons, which has necessarily lessened the consumption of stuffs; the low wages of the weavers and spinners, who are, in a considerable degree at the mercy of the manufacturers, and are not supposed to receive better pay than they did 20 years ago; and, lastly, to the war, which has put a stop to the exportation of stuffs to France, Flanders and Holland, and, from the high price of insurance, much reduced the trade to other countries. The merchants and manufacturers are now overstocked with goods; and the weavers are, consequently, very ill supplied with work, and, what is worse, are obliged to work up the worst materials.

Sir Frederick Morton Eden, *The State of the Poor*, 1797, vol. II, pp. 477–8

3.20 Proto-industry?

Merchants had in abundance sprung up, who rode from town to town, and valley to valley, to purchase these goods, which were mostly shipped to the continent of Europe. A new road to wealth had been opened – the farmer either forsook the tilling of the ground to follow altogether the stuff business, or else carried it on as a domestic employment along with the cultivation of the land, and with thrift habits, was often in an incredibly short time, enabled to purchase his homestead and farm . . .

John James, *History of the Worsted Manufacture in England from the Earliest Times*, 1857, p. 267

Questions

1 What evidence of the nature of manufacture does Defoe provide in document 3.17?
2 Both Young [3.18] and Eden [3.19] saw Norwich's worsted industry in a regional and European context. Explain what they mean by this and what its implications were for the development of the industry.
3 Explain Eden's analysis of why Norwich's industry declined.
4 John James [3.20] is a different type of source to Defoe, Young and Eden. What problems does this raise for historians?
5 What evidence for 'proto-industrialisation' can be found in documents 3.17–3.20?
6 'Capitalism predated industrialisation in textile manufacturing industries.' Discuss the validity of this statement.
7 What is the value of the notion of proto-industrialisation for historians of the 'industrial revolution'?

3.21   Towards a factory system

In the early days of textile manufactures, the locality of the factory depended upon the existence of a stream having a sufficient fall to turn a water-wheel; and, although the establishment of the water-mills was the commencement of the breaking-up of the domestic system of manufacture, yet the mills necessarily situated upon the streams, and frequently at considerable distances the one from the other, formed part of a rural, rather than an urban system; and it was not until the introduction of steam-power as a substitute for the stream that factories were congregated in towns, and localities where the coal and water required for the production of steam were found in sufficient quantities. The steam-engine is the parent of manufacturing towns.

A. Redgrave in *Reports of the Inspectors of Factories for the Half Year Ending 30 April 1860*, London, 1860, p. 36

3.22   A factory system

The term Factory System, in technology, designates the combined operation of many orders of work-people, adult and young, in tending with assiduous skill a series of productive machines continuously impelled by a central power. This definition includes such organisations as cotton-mills, flax-mills, silk-mills, woollen-mills and certain engineering works; but it excludes those in which the mechanisms do not form a connected series, nor are dependent on one prime mover. Of the latter class, examples occur in iron-works, dye-works, soap-works, brass-foundries . . . [the factory], in its strictest sense, involves the idea of a vast automaton, composed of various mechanical and intellectual organs acting in uninterrupted concert for the production of a common object, all of them being subordinated to a self-regulated moving force . . .

Andrew Ure, *The Philosophy of Manufactures*, London, 1835, pp. 13–14

Questions

1 How does Redgrave in 3.21 explain the evolution of the factory system?
2 How convincing do you find Redgrave's explanation of the emergence of factories? How would you relate this explanation to the notion of 'proto-industrialisation'?
3 Ure made a distinction between the 'factory system' and other forms of industrial production. What was the basis of his distinction and how convincing do you find it?
4 'The contemporary emphasis on the "factory" neglects other forms of manufacture.' What is your reaction to this statement?

5 Writers like Andrew Ure emphasised the economic benefits of factory production while Engels and others noted its social effects. Why was the contemporary debate on factories polarised and what effects did this have?

6 'The steam-engine is the parent of manufacturing towns.' [3.21] Why was Redgrave mistaken?

Historians have recently revised the traditional view of an 'industrial revolution'. Industrial change was not something that occurred simply after 1780 but took place over the whole of the eighteenth century. There was substantial growth in a whole range of traditional industries as well as in the obviously 'revolutionary' cases of iron and cotton. Technical change was not necessarily mechanisation but also the development of hand techniques and the wider use and division of labour. Change was the result of the conjunction of old and new processes. Steam power did not replace water power at a stroke. Work organisation was varied and even later than 1850 factories coexisted with domestic production, artisan workshops and large-scale mining and metal producing organisations. Change varied across industries and regions. To understand the economic revolutions of the eighteenth and nineteenth centuries historians must extend their vision of industrialisation beyond the conventional territories of cotton, iron and steam power and through their critique of change develop a broadened picture of Britain's economy.

4 A communications revolution

By 1750 Britain was already an exceedingly mobile and horse-drawn society. Travel may have been slow and, on occasions, dangerous but it was not uncommon. Cities like London and Norwich had their Welsh and Scottish societies. Within a hundred years the British, and especially the English, landscape was scarred by canals and railways and traversed by improved roads. Movement of goods and people was quickened dramatically by these innovations. Turnpike roads and the emergence of a sophisticated coaching 'industry', canals with their barges, new harbours, and the 'iron horse' all symbolised 'progress' as much as factories and enclosed fields.

However, just as historians now emphasise the persistence and importance of older manufacturing techniques and of the gradual improvement of existing farming methods, they have also drawn attention to the central role of existing methods of communication. It is important to question whether the notions of a 'Canal Age' and a 'Railway Age' are any longer of value.

This chapter will focus on the following aspects of this communications revolution. First, the reasons why improvements were necessary in the communications infrastructure will be considered. The remainder of the chapter will concentrate on railways. The 'technology' of railway improvement will be examined and the impact of railways on society will be assessed.

The need for 'improvement'

How bad were communications in the eighteenth century? There are many sources which point to the inadequacy of the road system and the inability of the authorities – since 1555, the local parishes – to maintain roads, and yet in 1637 Taylor's *Carriers' Cosmographie* revealed that an extensive network of carriers was already in being, linking London and the provinces. How far was it the existence of increased freight traffic in heavier four-wheeled wagons which created the communication problems? Why were parishes less willing to maintain the major roads crossed by these eighteenth-century juggernauts?

4.1   Condition of roads

In my journey to London, I travelled from Harborough to Northampton, and well was it that I was in a light Berlin, and six good horses, or I might have been overlaid in that turnpike road. But for fear of life and limb, I walked several miles on foot, met twenty waggons tearing their goods to pieces, and the drivers cursing and swearing for being robbed on the highway by a turnpike, screened under an act of Parliament.

Gentleman's Magazine, vol. XVII, 1747, p. 232

4.2   William Cowper on the wet season

I sing of a journey to Clifton
We would have performed if we could,
Without cart or barrow to life on
Poor Mary and me thro' the mud
Sle Sla Slud
Stuck in the mud
Oh it is pretty to wade through a flood
So away we went slipping and sliding
Hop, hop, à la mode de deux frogs. . . .

William Cowper, *The Distressed Travellers*, 1782

4.3   Statute labour: a major defect?

I have found by ten years' service in the office of a surveyor that five hired labourers will do as much work as ten or twelve who come out upon the statute. They make a holiday of it, lounge about, and trifle away their time. As they are in no danger of being turned out of their work, they stand in no awe of the surveyor. It is a common saying amongst us that if a drop of sweat should happen to fall from any of them it would infallibly produce a quagmire. In short, statute work will never mend the roads effectually.

From a minute book of a Shrewsbury parish surveyor writing in June 1788, quoted in M. Searle, *Turnpikes and Toll Bars*, vol. 1, London, 1930, p. 86

4.4   Improved roads: an engineer comments

To persons who were in the habit of travelling in Lanarkshire previous to these improvements, the change was surprising as well as gratifying; instead of roads cut into deep ruts through dangerous ravines, jolting the traveller, and injuring his carriage, – or leading him, if on horseback, plunging and staggering, circuitously over steep hills, the traveller has now smooth surfaces, with easy ascents, rendered safe by protecting fences. Such advantages being equally beneficial to all ranks of society, are of the first importance to a civilised nation.

The Life of Thomas Telford, Civil Engineer, written by himself, edited by John Rickman, 1838, quoted in H. Perkin, *The Age of the Railway*, 1970, p. 68

4.5   Improved roads: consequences

There never was a more astonishing revolution accomplished in the internal system of any country. The carriage of grain, coal, merchandize, etc., is in general conducted with little more than half of the number of horses which has guided all these movements, and upon which they turn, is the reformation which has been made in our public roads.

Henry Homer, *Enquiry into the Means of Preserving and Improving the Publick Roads*, 1767, quoted in H.J. Dyos and D.H. Aldcroft, *British Transport*, Leicester, 1971, p. 70

Questions

1 What, according to these sources, were the major defects in the English road system?
2 Assess the extent to which: (i) the technology of road construction; and (ii) statute labour were responsible for deficiencies in road communications. What other conditions led to deterioration in road conditions?
3 To what extent did turnpikes alone improve the road system? Use sources 4.1 and 4.5 as a basis for your answer. How far was the development of a coaching 'industry' necessary as well?
4 With reference to sources from other chapters of the book evaluate the extent to which roads inhibited short- and long-distance travel.
5 'Parochialism explains both the necessity for improving roads and the reasons why that improvement did not occur in any coherent manner.' Assess the validity of this statement.

The slowness of road travel meant that it was impossible to carry bulky goods like grain and coal very far and still sell them at a profit. The answer was water transport.

4.6   A late seventeenth-century view

Of necessity we must always be Sailing round the Island, carrying and recarrying such heavy Commodities from Port to Port, to be taken into the more Inward parts of the Kingdom, otherwise the charge of carrying such goods by Land, would rise to a very vast charge, the High-Ways of our Island being very uneven, and the ways therein in Winter time very bad.

Andrew Yarranton, *England's Improvement by Sea and Land*, 1698, vol. II, p. 92

4.7   Adam Smith on the advantages of water transport

As by means of water-carriage a more extensive market is opened to every sort of industry than what land-carriage alone can afford it, so it is upon the sea-coast, and along the banks of navigable rivers, that industry of every kind naturally begins to subdivide and improve itself, and it is frequently not till a long time after that those improvements extend themselves to the inland parts of the country. A broad-wheeled waggon, attended by two men, and drawn by eight horses, in about six weeks; time carries and brings back between London and Edinburgh near four ton weight of goods. In about the same time a ship navigated by six or eight men, and sailing between the ports of London and Leith, frequently carries and brings back two hundred ton weight of goods. Six or eight men, therefore, by the help of water-carriage, can carry and bring back in the same time the same quantity of goods between London and Edinburgh, as fifty broad-wheeled waggons, attended by a hundred men and drawn by four hundred horses . . . Were there no other communication between those two places, therefore, but by land-carriage, as no goods could be transported from the one to the other, except such whose price was very considerable in proportion to their weight, they could carry on but a small part of that commerce which at present subsists between them, and consequently could give but a small part of that encouragement which they at present mutually afford to each other's industry. There could be little or no commerce of any kind between the distant parts of the world. What goods could bear the expense of land-carriage between London and Calcutta?

Adam Smith, *An Inquiry into the Nature and Causes of the Wealth of Nations*, book 1, chapter 3, 1776 edited by Andrew Skinner, 1970, pp. 122–3

4.8   A carrier's attitude to canals, 1797

The Cannals now run very quick – Mr R. Hims wanted four piano Fortes down, two he ordered by canal, the other two by our wagon (as 2 of them were immediately wanted) those by Canal arrive 3 days before those by our wagon & were all delivered at the same time. Canal delivered them the 9th day, ours the

12th. The difference in ye carriage was 10/- more by us than those by canal . . . I trust and hope the Cannal doth not allways bate us in point of time or we shall be quiet don over. The Irish Tea & Hop merchants tells me they wonder how we get any Businefs as they pay Pickford no more than 6/-/P/cwt & I receive 9/6. As for the Irish linens I do all that lays in my power to get more but it is impossible whilst the canal . . . under carry us.

Letter from Lydia Sutton, a carrier's agent in Liverpool to her principal, James Holt, in London, printed in P.J.G. Ransom, *The Archaeology of the Transport Revolution 1750–1850,* **1984, p. 48. Their correspondence can be found in the Waterways Museum, Stoke Bruerne.**

4.9   The impact of improvement

Good roads, canals and navigable rivers, by diminishing the expense of carriage, put the remote parts of the country more nearly upon a level with those in the neighbourhood of the town. They are upon that account the greatest of all improvements. They encourage the cultivation of the remote, which must always be the most extensive circle of the country. They are advantageous to the town, by breaking down the monopoly of the country in its neighbourhood. They are advantageous even to that part of the country. Though they introduce some rival commodities into the old market, they open many new markets to its produce. Monopoly, besides, is a great enemy to good management, which can never be universally established but in the consequence of that free and universal competition which forces everybody to have recourse to it for the sake of self-defence. It is not more than fifty years ago that some of the counties in the neighbourhood of London petitioned the parliament against the extension of the turnpike roads into the remoter counties. Those remoter counties, they pretended, from the cheapness of labour, would be able to sell their grass and corn cheaper in the London market than themselves, and would thereby reduce their rents and ruin their cultivation. Their rents, however, have risen, and their cultivation has been improved since that time.

Adam Smith, *An Inquiry into the Nature and Causes of the Wealth of Nations,* **book 1, chapter 11, 1776, edited by Andrew Skinner, 1970, p. 251**

Questions

1 How far is the view of Andrew Yarranton [4.6] supported by Lydia Sutton [4.8] and in what ways? In what ways had water communications changed in the century between these two sources?
2 What is the basis of Adam Smith's view of water-carriage in 4.7?
3 In what ways did Smith [4.7 and 4.9] see deficient communications holding back the division of labour and economic improvement? How convincing do you find his case?

4 Lydia Sutton was in competition with Pickford. Smith contrasts 'competition' with 'monopoly' in **4.9**. What did he mean by this?

Smith may have sought competition in communications but by the early nineteenth century canals enjoyed an increasing monopoly for long-distance and heavy-goods haulage while roads were largely concerned with transporting people and goods of low weight and higher cost. Railways, initially a response to this situation [**4.10**], quickly established a monopoly of their own.

4.10   The Liverpool and Manchester Railway prospectus

The Committee of the Liverpool and Manchester Railway Company think it right to state, concisely, the grounds upon which they rest their claim to public encouragement and support. The importance, to a commercial state, of a safe and cheap mode of transit for merchandise from one part of the country to another, will be readily acknowledged. This was the plea, upon the first introduction of canals: it was for the public advantage; and although the new mode of conveyance interfered with existing and inferior modes, and was opposed to the feelings and prejudices of landowners, the great principle of the public good prevailed, and experience has justified the decision.

It is upon the same principle that railroads are now proposed to be established; as a means of conveyance manifestly superior to existing modes; possessing moreover this recommendation, in addition to what could have been claimed in favour of canals, namely, that the railroad scheme holds out to the public not only a cheaper, but far more expeditious conveyance than any yet established.

. . . The Committee are aware that it will not immediately be understood by the public how the proprietors of a railroad, requiring an invested capital of £400,000, can afford to carry goods at so great a reduction upon the charges of the present water companies . . . It is not that the water companies have not been able to carry goods on more reasonable terms, but that, strong in the enjoyment of their monopoly, they have not thought it proper to do so . . . IT IS COMPETITION THAT IS WANTED . . .

But it is not altogether on account of the exorbitant charges of the water-carriers that a railroad is desirable. The present canal establishments are inadequate to . . . the regular and punctual conveyance of goods at all periods and seasons. In summer time there is frequently a deficiency of water, obliging boats to go only half-loaded, while, in winter, they are sometimes locked up with frosts, for weeks together . . .

Amongst the widely-diffused benefits to be expected from the proposed railroad, must especially be enumerated, no inconsiderable advance in the commercial prosperity of Ireland. The latent energies of that country, her capabilities as a manufacturing power, will be developed by being brought into easy contact and communication with the manufacturing districts of this

Kingdom; whilst every article of her agricultural industry will experience an increased demand, from the cheapness and facility with which it will be introduced into the prosperous counties of Lancaster and York. In the present state of trade and of commercial enterprise dispatch is no less essential than economy. Merchandise is frequently brought across the Atlantic from New York to Liverpool in 21 days; while, owing to the various causes of delay above enumerated, good have in some instances been longer on their passage from Liverpool to Manchester . . .

Printed in T. Baines, *History of Liverpool*, 1852, pp. 601–3

Questions

1 What case is put forward in this document for the development of a railway from Liverpool to Manchester?
2 How convincing would you have found the case if you were: (i) a canal shareholder; (ii) a Manchester manufacturer; and (iii) an individual from the working population. Why?
3 'He would say that, wouldn't he?' How reliable do you think the case for railways made in the 1825 Prospectus is and why?
4 Source 4.10 makes a strong case for railways as a means of improving the Irish economy. What is the basis of this argument? How far did the economic development of Ireland between 1830 and 1850 bear out this case?

Parochial considerations also played an important part in demands for improvements in communications as these examples demonstrate.

4.11a   Attitudes to the London to Birmingham Railway, 1840

I [Thomas Bennett, the Duke of Bedford's steward at Woburn] met with Mr Elger [a Bedford builder] today at Bedford, and had some conversations with him as to this being a good time for selling Building Ground in Bedford or not . . . Mr Elger says that should the Railway go on, it is impossible to say what alterations may take place in the value of property in the Town; and upon the whole . . . he thinks that persons who can hold their property should not bring it into Market just at this time.

There was a meeting held yesterday about the Railway, and the project was most favourably entertained by the Meeting. Mr Whitbread [Bedford MP] advocates it most strenuously, and will offer every support he can, and so also do many other proprietors on or about the Line. I think that if Manchester people make up their minds that a second line of rail is required, they will carry it, and if Bedford does not take advantage of the Line, some other Town probably will.

Northampton at this time is a deplorable instance of refusing to have a great Line passing through or near a Town. They are just as much shut out from the great thoroughfare as Woburn is – with this difference, that Northampton might have had it and did not see the advantage, and now they would give anything to get it when they cannot.

Letter from Thomas Bennett to Charles Haedy (the Duke's Agent-in-Chief in London), 22 July 1840, printed in F.G. Cockman, *The Railway Age in Bedfordshire*, 1974, pp. 6–7

4.11b Bennett again

Mr P. [Theed Pearse, the Bedford solicitor] informs me that the York and the Direct Northern Lines are about to join, and thinks it is most probable the Girtford branch will come to St. Leonards [station]. . . .

I asked his opinion of it as a speculation to which he replied it would do the proprietors no good, and ruin the Navigation. He also expressed alarm at some obstruction likely to be formed to the passage of water in flood times by crossing the vale oftener than in his opinion was necessary.

I suggested if the Navigation and Mill interests could be satisfactorily arranged and cleared away, whether his opinion would remain the same. He said certainly not, that he had thought of such a thing but it appeared too visionary. I laughed, and as he is of a speculative turn, I said 'nothing in these days is too visionary'. I then stated to him my views and opinions as to the great effect to be produced by the complete drainage of the whole vale of the Ouse and the great local and public advantage to be gained by the increased extent of land to be brought into cultivation, causing a great demand for labour and increase of food . . . He said he had never looked at it in such a light but thought it a subject of very great importance, and one that ought not to drop without further enquiry and examination.

Letter from Bennett to Haedy, 6 December 1844, printed in F.G.Cockman, *The Railway Age in Bedfordshire*, p. 14

4.11c Contraction and expansion

Sir, In resuming the subject of the London & Manchester Railway let us consider a few of the advantages to be derived therefrom. First to the town of St Albans. Previous to the opening of the London & Birmingham Railway nearly 100 coaches passed through that town daily and there was also a considerable business doing in posting. Large sums of money were expended in the town and consequently it was in a flourishing state. After the opening of the railways, business vanished. The only inference therefore which we can draw is this – that so soon as the proposed line comes into operation the trade will not only return but increase in tenfold degree, and what previously prevented St Albans from becoming a manufacturing town but the want of a railroad? Independent of this it has many attractions – its ancient Abbey, the monument to [Francis] Bacon [the early seventeenth-century essayist and politician], the celebrated Holy Well, the Town Hall and various other buildings. The air is very salubrious and it is surrounded by the most picturesque scenery. With such advantages there would doubtless be a great increase in the inhabitants, for when it is brought within an hour's ride of the Metropolis the man of business will eagerly embrace the opportunity to remove to such a delightful spot. He will be enabled to arrive at his office in town in less than an hour from the time he leaves home, and can after the fatigues of the day return to his family in one of the most delightful spots imaginable. House rents will also be cheaper and the expense of the family be considerably diminished . . .

Letter from Q.E.D., printed in *The Reformer* (later called *The Hertford & Bedford Reformer*), 1 August 1840

Questions

1 What do these sources tell historians about individual motives for supporting railway promotion?
2 'Railways could lead to urban contraction as well as expansion.' In what ways do these sources support this assertion?
3 Why was the Duke of Bedford's steward at Woburn so concerned about railway development?
4 Railway development was as much about speculation as improving the economy. Why did Thomas Bennett see no contradiction between these two positions?
5 'Nothing in these days is too visionary.' [4.11b] What do you think Bennett meant by this? Consider his statement with reference to other sectors of the economy.
6 In 1907 the *Victoria County History for Essex* said that 'It was not easy to lay rails in the soft Essex soil and a good deal of the county is still untouched by railroads *and therefore* [author's italics] quietly unprogressive in spirit.' Discuss this conclusion.

The technology of improvement

Transport developed rapidly in the second half of the eighteenth century but remained dependent on traditional forms of power – animal, wind and manual. The prospect of making self-propelled steam boats and carriages was, however, attractive but, despite James Watt's improvements in the power of the steam engine, this did not really occur till after 1800. This section will examine attitudes to steam-powered propulsion and the problems of railway construction. In 1784 Watt took out a patent for a steam carriage. His motives for doing so are difficult to fathom. Certainly he doubted the ability of ironmasters to produce boilers capable of containing steam at high pressures but there may have been other motives [4.12]. This effectively ended any meaningful work on steam locomotion until 1800. Richard Trevithick and other engineers pioneered the early development of the steam locomotive but it was George Stephenson whom contemporaries remembered. The next set of documents looks at contrasting attitudes to steam locomotion.

4.12 Attitudes to steam locomotion: Watt to Boulton

[Building a steam carriage] will cost much time to bring it to any tolerable degree of perfection, and that for me to interrupt the career of our business to bestow attention on it would be imprudent.

Letter from James Watt to Matthew Boulton, his partner, printed in P.J.G. Ransom, *The Archaeology of the Transport Revolution 1750–1850*, 1984, pp. 73–4

4.13 Attitudes to steam locomotion: a dialogue

BILL: Good morning, Jack. I am glad I have met with you to bid you a good-bye, for I am going away for a while for you know there is a great deal of employment going forward in making these new Railroads.

JACK: Yes, Bill, the Railroads are something like the new Workhouses, make work at present for a few, and in the end be the ruin of a great many.

BILL: Why, Jack, steam is all the rage, steam boats, steam sawyers, steam bakers and millers, and I expect very soon we shall have to live upon steam.

JACK: No! No! Bill, you're mistaken, instead of living by steam it will prove a great help in taking away life, and numbers will be thrown out of employment, for I cannot see what benefit we shall derive from it.

BILL: Why, Jack, it may be a benefit to the town of Leicester, the London markets will be plentifully supplied with all kinds of corn, butter, cheese, eggs and stockings and from the Seaports fish alive on the dish.

JACK: Why we now see the Railroads a moving panorama of live lumber, like a string of Noah's Arks, filled with men and women, pigs, sheep and oxen carried by steam, cooked by steam and then devoured by steam.

BILL: And, Jack, it will be a fine chance for the Leicester bricklayers, they may now undertake to send ready built Workhouses by steam for the poor paupers of the different parishes from the North to the South of England; well secured with iron bars and cast iron roofs to keep them from escaping.

JACK: Why they tell me, Bill, that as there are no more coach horses wanted, they will be taken to the fellmonger's yard, there to be converted into hog's lard.

BILL: But what will become of the Innkeepers, Ostlers and Coach Proprietors?

JACK: Become of them! Why as they have always been fond of the horse line, they may now enlist in the line of Horses of her Majesty the great Queen of Spain or ride upon English donkeys for the good of their health.

BILL: Well, Jack, I must bid you good-bye at present for this job won't last always; for Shareholders, Engine scheme and all may yet be blown up by the boiler of hot water.

A Most Curious and Interesting Dialogue on the NEW RAIL ROADS*, Or, the delights and pleasures of Travelling by Hot Water.* It preceded the broadsheet of the ballad 'The Wonderful Effects of the Leicester Rail Road', published in 1836–7, printed in R. Palmer (ed.), *A Touch on the Times: Songs of Social Change 1770 to 1914*, 1974, pp. 52–5

Questions

1 In what ways does source 4.13 give a slanted view of attitudes to steam locomotion?

2 Discuss the tone of source 4.13. In what senses can it be said to be propaganda?

3 In what ways does the dialogue [4.13] reflect contemporary concerns about the advantages and disadvantages of the railways?

4 How far and why did James Watt obstruct the development of steam locomotion?

The publication of a prospectus advertising the intention to promote a company was the first stage in railway construction. A provisional committee would then have a Bill introduced in Parliament to create a company empowered to purchase land and contract for constructing the line and allowed to raise the necessary funds by issuing shares. Opposition from local landowners could be vociferous. The London to Birmingham line missed Northampton because of the energetic tactics of the Duke of Grafton and Sir William Wake [4.11a]. The principal landowners of the Isle of Wight were able to delay the first railway on the island from 1845 to 1862. In a letter to the *Hampshire Telegraph* five leading landowners wrote:

4.14 Opposition

Possessors of property to the amount of 76,000 acres [were against the projected line in 1845 and its only supporters were] possessors of about 8,000 acres . . . Our answer is we don't want your plan. It is not a question of which direction your lines may take; we say, and we declare publicly that we don't require and we won't have *any* railways on this island.

Letter to the editor, 1 July 1845, quoted in P.S. Bagwell, *The Transport Revolution from 1770*, 1974, p. 126

Once railways came the area became extremely popular as a holiday resort and it was commercial rather than landed interests that determined the island's future development.

4.15   Disraeli on aristocratic inconsistency

'You came by the railroad?' enquired Lord de Mowbray mournfully, of Lady Marney.
'From Marham, about ten miles from us,' replied her ladyship.
'A great revolution?'
'Isn't it.'
'I fear it has a dangerous tendency to equality,' said his Lordship, shaking his head; 'I suppose Lord Marney gives them all the opposition in his power?'
'There is nobody so violent against the railroads as George,' said Lady Marney, 'I cannot tell you what he does not do! He organised the whole of our division against our Marham line.'
'I rather counted on him,' said Lord de Mowbray, 'to assist me in resisting this joint branch here; but I was surprised to learn that he had consented.'
'Not until the compensation was settled,' innocently remarked Lady Marney: 'George never opposes them after that. He gave up all opposition to the Marham line when they agreed to his terms.'
'And yet', said Lord de Mowbray, 'I think if Lord Marney would take a different view of the case, and look to the moral consequences, he would not hesitate. Equality, Lady Marney, equality is not our metier. If we nobles do not make a stand against the levelling spirit of the age, I am at a loss to know who will fight the battle. You may depend upon it these railroads are very dangerous things.'

Benjamin Disraeli, *Sybil*, 1845, Oxford, 1926, p. 153

Questions

1 These two sources give different explanations for opposition to railways. What are they?
2 'The attitude of the landed interest to railways was ambiguous.' In what ways do these sources support this assertion?

3 'I fear it has a dangerous tendency towards equality.' [4.15] How far did railways have a 'levelling' influence?

4 'Opposition to railways was concerned as much with social as economic issues.' Discuss.

Until the 1850s, when some steam-driven equipment was introduced, railways were built by hand and dynamite by the railway navvies. The following two extracts give differing views of construction, while the statistics provide an indication of the employment potential of railways.

4.16   'Railway navigators'

The improvident habits of the class of men known as navigators are alluded to in a report to the Poor Law Commissioners appended to the fifth report of the Select Committee on Railways. It appears that, during the winter of 1842, as many as fourteen of these persons were admitted in one night into the Abingdon Workhouse. It is stated that they usually receive wages varying from 3/- to 4/6d for every ten hours' labour, but are required by their gang of fellow workmen to subscribe to a gallon of beer daily and another gallon at the time the ganger or sub-contractor pays their wages. As the works approach completion employment is difficult to obtain, and then the labourers, having previously spent their earnings in the most lavish manner, undergo severest privations, frequently subsisting for a whole week upon the wages of a single day. Ultimately there is no longer any prospect of employment upon that particular undertaking and then the workmen remove, seeking shelter and food in the Union workhouses on their route, to some other locality where employment is more abundant.

The Railway Record, 3 August 1844

4.17   Thomas Brassey at work

When Mr Brassey took any contract, he let out portions of the work to sub-contractors. His way of dealing with them was this: he generally furnished all the materials, and all the plant. I find him on one occasion ordering as many as 2,400 waggons from Messrs Ransome & May. He also provided the horses. The sub-contractors contracted for the manual work alone . . . I find that the sub-contracts varied from £5,000 to £25,000; and that the number of men employed upon them would be from one to three hundred – the former being more common than the latter . . . Mr Brassey's mode of dealing with the sub-contractors was of an unusual kind, and such as could not have been adopted except by a man who had great experience of all kinds of manual work, and who was also a very just man . . .

Arthur Helps, *The Life and Labours of Mr Brassey*, 1872, pp. 47–9

4.18   Table showing number of staff employed on the railways of Britain on 1 May 1848

	Lines open	Under construction
Labourers	14,297	147,087
Artificers	10,814	29,087
Porters and messengers	7,559	10
Platelayers	4,391	256
Clerks	4,360	887
Policemen	2,475	71
Engine-stokers	1,809	—
Engine-drivers	1,752	—
Guards	1,464	—
Switchmen	1,058	—
Foremen or overseers	1,010	685
Gatekeepers	401	—
Superintendants	343	1,897
Miscellaneous	197	
Waggoners	141	—
Storekeepers	125	243
Draughtsmen	106	306
Engineers	95	405
Secretaries	81	102
Accountants	70	145
Cashiers	48	88
Brakesmen	32	—
Managers	30	93
Treasurers	29	21
Miners or quarrymen	—	6,250
Inspectors	—	119
Drivers and carters	—	45
Land surveyors	—	26
TOTALS	52,687	188,071

On this date 4,253 miles were open for traffic, 2,958 miles were under construction.

From C. Harvie, *The Industrialisation Process 1830–1914*, 1971, p. 62

Questions

1 Assess the value of source 4.16 to historians of railway construction.
2 What can you learn about the construction of railways from source 4.17?
3 'The employment potential of railways lay in their construction rather than their operation.' Discuss the validity of this assertion in relation to source 4.18.
4 How far did the development of railways to 1850 complement existing communication networks?

The impact of railways

From 1830 railways were *the* epoch-making transport innovation. Their economic significance lay in their ability to handle both major categories of traffic – goods and people – which no other single mode of transport had previously been able to do. Railways offered both lower costs and greater speed. Surprisingly it was the speed that attracted passengers, mail and high value goods. Mail went to new railways within six months and coaches running in direct competition swiftly lost their clientele and were run off the road. But the rival waterways were able, through cutting their rates and improving their services, to continue to win goods for several years. In 1840 the volume of goods carried by water from Liverpool to Manchester was more than twice as great as that carried by railway. Horse-drawn transport was also not immediately eclipsed by the steam railway. By encouraging economic growth railways generated short-distance horse-drawn transport to and from stations as well as stimulating local traffic in rural areas. In urban areas the movement of passengers and goods was almost entirely in horse-drawn vehicles. It has been estimated that there were 251,000 horses involved in transport in 1811, but this had risen to 264,000 by 1851 and to over a million by 1901.

Historians today do not have the confidence of the Victorians, who had little hesitation in assuming a direct relationship between railways and economic growth. But there is little doubting their social and cultural impact. This view is supported by the statistics: 64,000 travellers in 1843 but 174,000 in 1848, with an increase in the third-class element from 19,000 to 86,000 in the same period. The Great Exhibition of 1851 reinforced this increased mobility of population. *The Illustrated London News* [4.19] and Alexander Somerville [4.20] provide two views of the contemporary wonder of railways. The inscription from Ely cathedral [4.21] commemorating the deaths of William Pickering and Richard Edger in a railway accident expresses Victorian attitudes to the railway.

4.19 A newspaper comments in 1850

'The people', popularly so called, have been enabled thanks to railways and to the organisation of cheap pleasure-trips, to indulge in travels to distances which their forefathers had neither time nor money to undertake . . . Now travelling bids fair to become not only the necessity of the rich, but the luxury of the poor. The great lines of railways in England, by granting facilities for 'monster' or excursion trains at cheaper rates, have conferred a boon upon the public . . .

The Illustrated London News, September 1850

4.20 Alexander Somerville

But the distance between the separated classes of society, and the distance between the opponent ranks of industry, are reduced as intercourse is enlarged. The locomotive does more than subdue the space between town and town – it lessens the space between man and man; and gives them newer thoughts the closer that they come together. While it is yet the sleeping time of night, its other steam at the printing press, labours as if each piston stroke was an impulse of its great heart to enlarge the minds of the human millions, for whom, while the sun is also rising, the locomotive shall carry away to all points of the geographic compass, through all sections of the social scale, the knowledge which the press has multiplied in the mind. Each new subjugator of time and geographic distance, be it steam, strong enough to mingle the population of cities and shires in one corporeal admixture; or electricity fleet enough to snatch up a thought, leave it a hundred miles away and return for another ere the birth-time of the next – each is a subjugator of enmities and social distances . . . To those who advocated the reform of 1832, it may be almost deemed a triumph, to have lived to see it has done no harm. The opposition to it was not founded upon the probability of its doing no good, but on the certainty of its doing positive and irreparable mischief . . . The first principle of magnitude – the greatest of all, indeed, solved by the establishment of the Manchester and Liverpool Railway, was this, that the *innovation* upon old customs was safe. The railways have proved that, and much more . . . The time when I first saw the railway unite Liverpool and Manchester – spanning the bog where human foot could never tread – stands as I have said, in memory, like an epoch of my life. I looked upon the most poetical and most practical of the grand achievements of human intellect, until people thought I stood and slept; and; when they heard the dream, they said it was dreamy indeed. I should fear to tell the dreams which I have now besides the electric telegraph, and on the railways, and within the regions of the god-like inventions and makers of machinery. There is a time coming when realities shall go beyond any dreams that have yet been told of those things. Nation exchanging with nation their goods freely; thoughts exchanging themselves with thoughts, and never taking note of the geographical space they have to pass over, except to give the battery a little more of the electric spirit . . . Universal enfranchisement, railways, electric

telegraphs, public schools (the greatest of the moral levers for elevating mankind
named last – because last to be advocated, which should have been first); these
are some of the elements of a moral faith, believing in the universal brotherhood
of mankind, which I daily hold, and never doubt upon; which I believe will as
certainly be realised, as I believe that good, and not evil, was the object of all
creation and is the end of all existence.

**Alexander Somerville, *The Autobiography of a Working Man*, 1848,
Fitzroy edition, 1967, pp. 121, 246–7**

4.21   Technology and religion: 'The Spiritual Railway'

The line to heaven by Christ was made
With heavenly truth the rails were laid
From Earth to Heaven the line extends
To Life Eternal where it ends
Repentance is the Station then
Where passengers are taken in
No Fee for them is there to pay
For Jesus is Himself the way
God's Word is the first Engineer
It points the way to Heaven so clear
Through tunnels dark and dreary here
It does the way to Glory steer
God's Love the Fire, his Truth the Steam
Which drives the Engine and the Train.
All those who would to Glory ride
Must come to Christ, in Him abide
In First and Second and Third Class,
Repentance, Faith and Holiness
You must the way to Glory gain
Or you with Christ will not remain
Come the poor Sinners, now's the time
At any Station of the Line
If you'll repent and turn from Sin
The train will stop and take you in.

**Memorial in Ely Cathedral commemorating the deaths of two railway
workers**

Questions

1 These sources provide alternative perspectives on the impact of the
  railways. What were they?

2 How is it possible to say that **4.19** was written for a middle-class audience and **4.20** for the working population?

3 Why did Somerville [**4.20**] draw a parallel between the 1832 Reform Act and the development of the railways?

4 How successful do you think Somerville is in his emphasis on the moral power of 'new' technology? Justify your response.

5 What do you think the appeal of 'The Spiritual Railway' [**4.21**] would have been to a mid nineteenth-century audience and why?

6 Does **4.21** tell the historian more about spiritual or technological values and why?

Between 1750 and 1850 greater output was achieved by the communication system, as in manufacturing industry, by applying a rapidly increasing labour force to existing and frequently better organised modes of production, as well as by using new techniques and applying steam-driven machinery. Though emphasis has been placed on railways and the *new* technology in this chapter, historians are beginning to draw attention to the survival and the spread of older methods of communication. Coastal and river traffic became increasingly important and the horse remained the staple means of road transportation well beyond 1850. Steam power did not immediately eclipse older forms of traction.

5 A revolution in trade

Daniel Defoe observed in his *A Plan of English Commerce* that, 'the sum of all improvements in trade [was] the finding out some markets for the sale or vent of merchandize, where there was no sale or vent of goods before'. His statement draws attention to the crucial characteristic of trade in pre-industrialised economies. Merchants could only make significant increases in their sales by capturing more of the market from their rivals and were unlikely to achieve this through competitive reductions in prices by cost-cutting innovations in transport or manufacture. In international trade therefore commerce seemed a continuous fight over markets of limited size with England increasing its share of the market only at the expense of others' losses. It meant that the intense Anglo-Dutch rivalry was followed by rivalry with France. The period between the onset of the first Anglo-Dutch war in 1651 and the end of the Seven Years War in 1763 was an age of trade wars and trade treaties. It resulted in the emergence of Britain as *the* dominant commercial power in the international commercial world and the possessor of the largest mercantile marine in Europe.

This chapter considers two major aspects of trade. First, the changing patterns of Britain's international trade and the nature of the 'commercial revolution' will be considered through an examination of available statistics. This will be followed by a discussion of the nature of internal trade and the role of the consumer.

Changing patterns of trade

Compared to other areas of economic activity in the eighteenth century statistics relating to overseas trade are relatively abundant. Fairly reliable data on imports, exports and re-exports are available from the late seventeenth century. There are, however, problems with the statistics available. For what purpose were they compiled and how accurate were they? How far do they take into account the widespread evasion of customs duties? What was the impact of smuggling?

5.1 Henry Martin on the value of official statistics

If the thing intended by these valuations was to discover at one view the increase or decrease of the quantitys of goods, imported or exported, it must be acknowledged that the keeping always to the same price of the same species of goods serves best for this purpose, since the increase or decrease of the quantitys must show at once in some measure this last increase or decrease; whereas if it had been possible to have bought into the total values the numberless variations of prices of all sorts of goods, this had not been sufficient to show the increase and decrease of the quantitys imported or exported, since it often happens that a less quantity of goods in one year is of more value than a greater of the same goods in another.

Henry Martin, 'Observations upon the Account of Exports and Imports for 17 Years', 1718, printed in G.N. Clark, *Guide to English Commercial Statistics, 1696–1782*, 1938, p. 63

Questions

1 What was the main argument Henry Martin put forward in this document?
2 In what ways does Martin counsel caution in using official trade figures?
3 What is the importance of Martin as a source for historians of trade in this period?

5.2 Table showing English trade 1700–1799 (£m)

	Imports	Exports	Re-exports	Exports and re-exports
1700–9	4.7	4.5	1.7	6.1
1710–19	5.5	4.8	2.1	6.9
1720–9	6.8	4.9	2.8	7.7
1730–9	7.5	5.8	3.2	9.0
1740–9	7.3	6.5	3.6	10.1
1750–9	8.4	8.7	3.5	12.2
1760–9	10.8	10.0	4.4	14.4
1770–9	12.1	9.3	5.1	14.4
1780–9	13.8	10.2	4.3	14.5
1790–9	21.8	17.5	9.4	26.9

From E.B. Schumpeter, *English Overseas Trade Statistics 1697–1808*, Oxford, 1960, pp. 15–16 and B.R. Mitchell and P. Deane, *Abstract of British Historical Statistics*, Cambridge, 1962, pp. 279–83

5.3   Table showing English and Welsh imports (in £m)

		1699–1701	*1772–4*
Raw materials	Silk, raw and thrown	346	751
	Flax and hemp	194	581
	Wool	200	102
	Cotton	44	137
	Textile yarn	232	424
	Dyes	226	506
	Iron and steel	182	481
	Timber	138	319
	Oil	141	162
	Tallow	85	131
	Miscellaneous	248	607
	TOTALS	2,036	4,201
Foodstuffs	Wine	536	411
	Spirits	10	205
	Sugar	630	2,364
	Tobacco	249	519
	Fruit	174	159
	Pepper	103	33
	Drugs	53	203
	Tea	8	848
	Coffee	27	436
	Rice	5	340
	Corn	—	398
	Miscellaneous	174	561
	TOTALS	1,969	6,477
Manufactures	Linens	903	1,274
	Calicoes	367	697
	Silks and mixed fabrics	208	82
	Metalwares	72	7
	Thread	79	14
	Miscellaneous	215	111
	TOTALS	1,844	2,185
	TOTAL IMPORTS	5,849	12,863

From R. Davis, 'English foreign trade 1700–1774', in W.E. Minchinton (ed.), *The Growth of English Overseas Trade in the 17th and 18th centuries*, 1969, pp. 119–20

5.4   Table showing English and Welsh exports and re-exports (in £m)

		1699–1701	*1772–4*
Exports			
Raw materials	Lead	128	182
	Tin	97	116
	Coal	35	333
	Miscellaneous	102	163
	TOTAL	362	794
Foodstuffs	Grain	147	37
	Fish	190	70
	Hops	9	136
	Miscellaneous	102	329
	TOTALS	448	572
Manufactures	Woollens	3,045	4,186
	Linens	—	740
	Silks	80	189
	Cottons, etc.	20	221
	Metalware	114	1,198
	Hats	45	110
	Miscellaneous	279	1,843
	TOTALS	3,583	8,487
	TOTAL EXPORTS	4,393	9,853
Re-exports			
Raw materials	Dyestuffs	85	211
	Silk	63	125
	Miscellaneous	151	378
	TOTALS	299	714
Foodstuffs	Tobacco	421	904
	Sugar	287	429
	Pepper	93	110
	Tea	2	295
	Coffee	2	873
	Rice	4	363
	Rum	—	199
	Drugs	48	132
	Miscellaneous	84	237
	TOTALS	941	3,542

Table 5.4 (*cont.*)

		1699–1701	*1772–4*
Manufactures	Calicoes	340	701
	Silks, etc.	150	501
	Linens	182	322
	Miscellaneous	74	38
	TOTALS	746	1,562
	TOTAL RE-EXPORTS	1,986	5,818
	TOTAL EXPORTS AND RE-EXPORTS	6,379	15,671

Ibid., pp. 119–20

5.5   Table showing geographical distribution of English and Welsh trade (as percentages)

	1700–1	*1750–1*	*1772–3*
Imports from:			
Europe	66	55	45
North America	6	11	12
West Indies	14	19	25
East Indies and Africa	14	15	18
Re-exports to:			
Europe	85	79	82
North America	5	11	9
West Indies	6	4	3
East Indies and Africa	4	5	6
Domestic exports to:			
Europe	85	77	49
North America	6	11	25
West Indies	5	5	12
East Indies and Africa	4	7	14

From P. Deane, *The First Industrial Revolution*, Cambridge, 1965, p. 56

Questions

1 What different sorts of information can historians obtain from these statistical sources?
2 What trading issues do they leave unanswered?
3 In what respects did the nature of: (i) imports; (ii) exports; and (iii) re-exports alter between 1700 and 1775? What significance do you attach to each of these alterations?
4 In what respects did the relationship between imports, exports and re-exports change during this period? Why do you think these changes occurred?
5 In what ways did the geographical distribution of trade change between 1700 and 1775? Why did this change occur?
6 What evidence do these statistics provide for a 'commercial revolution'?
7 What do you think a 'commercial revolution' meant to contemporaries?

5.6 Table showing structure of the domestic export trade 1750–1850 (as a percentage of total exports)

	1750	*1770*	*1800*	*1830*	*1850*
Coal, coke, etc.	1.6	2.7	2.0	0.5	1.8
Grain	19.6	—	—		—
Fish	1.0	1.0	1.0	1.1	1.0
Iron/steel goods	5.2	7.0	5.8	10.2	12.3
Cotton	0.2	2.0	24.1	50.8	39.6
Wool/worsted	45.6	43.4	28.4	12.7	14.1
Linen	2.4	4.5	3.3	5.4	6.8
Silk	1.2	1.4	1.2	1.4	1.5

Textile figures include both yarn and manufactures. Figures for 1770 and after are for England, Wales and Scotland. The 1750 figures are for England and Wales alone.

From P. Deane and W.A. Cole, *British Economic Growth 1688–1959*, Cambridge, 2nd edition, 1967, p. 31 and E. Pawson, *The Early Industrial Revolution*, 1978, p. 220

5.7   Table showing structure of British imports 1770–1830 (percentage of total value)

	1770	*1800*	*1810*	*1820*	*1830*
Corn	3	5	5	5	3
Other food	32	35	42	41	35
Textile raw materials	16	15	19	26	33
Other raw materials	6	4	6	8	10
Miscellaneous	43	41	28	20	19

From B.R. Mitchell and P. Deane, *Abstract of British Historical Statistics*, Cambridge, 1962, pp. 285–9

5.8   Table showing geographical distribution of British export trade by continent (as percentage of total value)

	1816–18	*1836–8*	*1849–51*
Europe	44.2	41.1	38.0
Africa	1.0	3.6	3.8
Asia	8.3	11.3	14.8
North America	37.3	21.2	24.5
South America	9.3	20.7	16.0
Australasia	—	2.2	3.6

From W. Schlote, *British Overseas Trade from 1700 to the 1930s*, Oxford, 1952, pp. 156–8

Questions

1 What information can historians obtain from documents **5.6–5.8** to explain Britain's growing trade?
2 In what ways did the nature of imports and exports change between 1770 and 1850? Why did these changes occur?
3 In what ways did the geographical distribution of trade change in the first half of the nineteenth century? Why did this occur?
4 'Britain – the workshop of the world.' In what ways do these sources support this assertion?
5 How far did changes in other sectors of the economy affect British trade between 1780 and 1850?
6 Using sources **5.2–5.8** assess the extent to which Britain's growth in

trade was linked with colonial possessions. Did imperialism and trade growth go hand in hand?

5.9   Table showing balance of trade 1800–50

	(a)	(b)	(c)	(d)	(e)	(f)
1801–05	47.9	39.9	− 8.0			
1806–10	54.0	42.9	−11.8			
1811–15	50.4	42.9	− 7.5			
1816–20	49.3	40.3	− 9.0	14.5	1.7	7.2
1821–25	45.4	37.3	− 8.1	14.2	4.2	10.3
1826–30	48.7	35.9	−12.8	10.6	4.6	2.6
1831–35	53.6	40.4	−13.1	14.1	5.4	6.4
1836–40	73.8	49.8	−24.0	18.6	8.0	2.6
1841–45	71.0	54.0	−17.0	15.4	7.5	5.9
1846–50	87.7	60.9	−26.8	22.0	9.5	4.7

(a)   annual average of net imports in £m at current prices
(b)   annual averages of net exports of UK products in £m at current prices
(c)   balance of commodity trade: (c)=(b)−(a)
(d)   net income from services, including shipping credits, insurance, banking, emigrant funds, tourist spending, profits from foreign trade etc. in £m
(e)   net income from interest and dividends in £m
(f)   balance of trade in £m: (f)=(c)+(d)+(e)

From A.H. Imlah, *Economic Elements in the Pax Britannica*, Oxford, 1958, pp. 37–8, 70–5, 94–8

Questions

1 What information about British trade can historians extract from document **5.9**?
2 In what ways does the evidence in **5.9** support or contradict **5.6–5.8**?
3 Explain the trends in Britain's balance of trade between 1800 and 1850.
4 'The official values for trade give an optimistic picture of British manufacturing potential. An examination of the balance of trade calls that optimism into question.' Discuss this statement.
5 'Any examination of a commercial revolution before 1850 that neglects "invisible exports" will give a false picture of the prosperity of Britain's economy.' What are your reactions to this statement?

COLEG MENAI
BANGOR, GWYNEDD LL57 2TP

A consumer revolution?

By 1750 Britain already had a highly market-oriented economy. Imports, whether smuggled or legal, were moved quickly to market. Domestic goods, both agricultural and manufactured, were bought and sold directly at the network of markets or through 'middlemen' who acted as a conduit between producer and consumer. The market orientation, for example, of agriculture is evident in about 800 market towns in England and Wales alone. These markets were not evenly distributed: southern England had a rather denser network than elsewhere, while in the north, Wales and Scotland, market areas were more extensive. This reflected both the intensity of production and also market specialisation. Defoe constantly recorded the specialisation of both regions and markets in his *Tour* published in the mid 1720s. This can be seen in the movement of goods to London. Between June 1767 and June 1768 16,000 sheep, 14,000 cattle, 21,000 single horses and 24,000 animals in draught passed through the Birdlip Hill Turnpike Trust in Gloucestershire en route from south Wales to London. During the eighteenth century imports of coal into London rose from about one million to nearly three million tons per year. There seems little doubt that satisfying consumer demands was a key function of the economic system.

5.10a   Social attitudes: an English perspective

It is said of England, by way of distinction, and we all value ourselves upon it, that it is a trading country; and King Charles II . . . used to say, 'That the tradesmen were the only gentry in England' . . . two things I offer from that head.

First, our tradesmen are not, as in other countries, the meanest of our people.

Secondly, some of the greatest and best, and most flourishing families, among not the gentry only, but even the nobility, have been raised from trade, owe their beginning, their wealth, and their estates, to trade; and, I may add,

Thirdly, those families are not at all ashamed of their original, and indeed, have no occasion to be ashamed of it . . . Trade is so far here from being inconsistent with a gentleman, that, in short, trade in England makes gentlemen, and has peopled this nation with gentlemen . . .

Daniel Defoe, *The Complete English Tradesman*, London, 1726, Alan Sutton edition, 1987, pp. 212–13, 216

5.10b   Social attitudes: a continental perspective

Commerce, which has enriched English citizens, has helped to make them free, and this freedom in its turn has extended commerce, and that has made the greatness of the nation. Commerce has gradually established the naval forces thanks to which the English are masters of the seas . . . Posterity will perhaps learn with surprise that a small island which has no resources of its own except a little lead, some tin, some fuller's earth and coarse wool has through its commerce become powerful to send, in 1723, at one and the same time, three fleets to three extremities of the world . . . All this makes an English merchant justifiably proud and leads him to venture to compare himself, not without some reason, to a Roman citizen. And so the younger son of a Peer of the Realm does not look down on trade. Lord Townshend, Minister of State, has a brother who is happy to be a business man in the City. When Lord Oxford governed England, his younger brother was a factor at Aleppo, whence he refused to return and where he died.

This custom, which however is unfortunately beginning to disappear, seems monstrous to Germans who are mad about their quarterings; they cannot understand that the son of a Peer of England may only be a rich and influential bourgeois, whereas in Germany everybody is a Prince . . .

In France anyone is a Marquis who wants to be, and . . . loftily despises a business man and the business man so often hears people speak disparagingly of his profession that he is foolish enough to blush . . .

Voltaire, *Letters on England*, Penguin edition, 1980, pp. 51–2. The *Letters* were originally published in France in 1734 and reflect Voltaire's three years' exile in England between 1726 and 1729.

Questions

1 In what ways did Defoe and Voltaire agree with each other about social attitudes in England towards trade? Why do you think there is a significant degree of agreement?
2 Voltaire had only a limited understanding of the English economy. Why do you think this was the case?
3 How far was Voltaire using English attitudes as a means to attack continental attitudes? Why should he do this?
4 Why did Charles II say that 'tradesmen were the only gentry in England'? [5.10a] What did he mean by this?
5 How accurately did Defoe and Voltaire reflect English social attitudes towards trade?
6 'Social attitudes can explain whether an economy develops or stagnates.' Examine this statement with reference to the century after 1750.

The eighteenth and first half of the nineteenth centuries saw growing demands for consumer goods. Many of the marketing methods used today have their origins in this period: circulars, advertisements and 'special offers'. The causes of this commercialisation of society and its impact are matters of some disagreement among historians. Certainly, growing consumption influenced, and was in turn influenced by, trade and economic growth. But the meanings of consumption patterns are more complex and there were certainly limits to consumption. Possessing and using domestic goods enhanced status or displayed social rank. Social emulation played an important role, though whether Harold Perkin's argument that the key to industrial growth was 'the infinitely elastic home demand for mass consumer goods . . . and the key to that demand was social emulation . . . the compulsive urge for imitating the spending habits of one's betters' is open to question. There is also considerable doubt as to whether lower food prices stimulated a consumer boom. There were many reasons why people wanted to own material goods: some were practical, some financial, others psychological. It is important therefore to address the idea of a consumer society with care. The following questions are important in this process. *Who* were the 'consumers'? *What* goods were being consumed? *Why* did these people wish to spend their money (whether savings or normal expenditure) on these goods? *How* were they persuaded to spend their money?

5.11a   Henry Fielding, 1750

Nothing has wrought such an alteration in this order of people, as the introduction of trade. This hath indeed given a new face to the whole nation, hath in great measure subverted the former state of affairs, and hath almost totally changed the manners, customs and habits of the people, more especially of the lower sort. The narrowness of their future is changed into wealth; their frugality into luxury, their humility into pride, and their subjection into equality . . . while the Noblemen will emulate the Grandeur of a Prince and the Gentleman will aspire to the proper state of a Nobleman; the Tradesman steps from behind his Counter into the vacant place of the Gentleman. Nor doth the confusion end there: It reaches to the very Dregs of the People, who aspire still to a degree beyond that which belongs to them.

Henry Fielding, 'Enquiry into the Causes of the Late Increase of Robbers', 1750, printed in *Works*, vol. II, pp. 782–3

5.11b   British magazine, 1763

The present rage of imitating the manners of high life hath spread so far among the gentlefolks of lower life, that in a few years we shall probably have no common folk at all.

***British Magazine*, vol. IV, 1763, p. 417**

5.11c Josiah Tucker

Were an inventory to be taken of Household Goods and Furniture of a Peasant, or Mechanic, in France, and of a Peasant or Mechanic in England, the latter would be found on average to exceed the former in Value by at least three to one . . . [English manufacturers] are more adapted for the demands of Peasants or Mechanics, in order to appear in warm circumstances, for Farmers, Freeholders, Tradesmen and Manufacturers in Middling Life; and for Wholesale Dealers, and for all persons of Landed Estates to appear in genteel life; than for the Magnificence of Palaces or the Cabinets of Princes. Thus it is . . . that the English of those several denominations have better Conveniences in their Houses . . .

R.L. Schuyler, *Josiah Tucker: A Selection from his Economic and Political Writings*, 1931, printed in N. McKendrick, J. Brewer and J.H. Plumb, *The Birth of a Consumer Society*, 1983, pp. 25–6

5.11d David Macpherson, 1805

The home trade is with good reason believed to be a vast deal greater in value than the whole of the foreign trade, the people of Great Britain being the best customers to the manufacturers and trades of Great Britain.

D. Macpherson, *Annals of Commerce*, 1805, vol. III, p. 340

Questions

1 What support do these sources provide for historians who place an emphasis on social emulation as *the* cause for a consumer revolution?
2 Contemporaries equated social emulation with 'equality'. What did they mean by this and why did it concern them?
3 In what ways does the extract from Voltaire [5.10b] help to explain Josiah Tucker's [5.11c] comparison between England and France?
4 Assess the validity of David Macpherson's assertion about the role of the home trade.
5 Samuel Johnson argued that 'you cannot spend in luxury without doing good to the poor'. How far was there a democratisation of consumption: (i) between 1750 and 1800; and (ii) from 1800 to 1850?
6 'Materialism was a luxury only those with spare money could afford. For the poor materialism was about survival.' Discuss.

5.12a   Scottish attitudes

In their general habits the husbandmen [farmers] of those days were a sober, a frugal, and an industrious race. Though not averse to indulge occasionally in convivial sociality with their friends and neighbours, yet the leading tendency of their minds was parsimony and thrift.

John Robertson, *Rural Recollections; or The Progress of Improvement in Agriculture and Rural Affairs*, 1829, pp. 232–3

5.12b

Through out gentry lived plainly and frugally in common, yet upon certain occasions they wished to make a show . . . It was at marriages, christenings and burials, particularly the last, that country gentlemen were wont to exceed the bounds of moderation.

Alexander Ramsey, *Scotland and Scotsmen in the Eighteenth Century*, London, 1888, vol. II, pp. 73–4

Questions

1 What attitudes to consumption in Scotland are contained in these two documents?
2 In what ways do they contrast with sources **5.11a–d**?
3 Why do you think that there were differences between attitudes in England and Scotland?
4 'The "consumer revolution", like revolutions in other sectors of the economy, *only* has meaning when considered regionally.' Discuss this statement.

Contemporaries were aware that a revolution in shopping was taking place. 'Persuasion' was exerted on the consumer through advertisements, circulars and window displays in the major cities. A distinction quickly emerged between legitimate forms of advertising and 'puffing'. Johnson announced in 1761 that, 'advertisements are now so numerous that they are very negligently perused, and it is therefore become necessary to gain attention by eloquence sometimes sublime and sometimes pathetic'. By 1800 many contemporaries admitted both the variety of 'puffs' and their effectiveness. Johnson had earlier said that customers 'catch from example the contagion of desire'.

5.13 A continental perspective on shopping in London, 1786

Behind the great glass windows absolutely everything one can think of is neatly, attractively displayed, in such abundance of choice as almost to make one greedy. Now large slipper and shoe shops for anything from adults down to dolls, can be seen, now fashion-articles or silver or brass shops, books, guns, glasses, the confectioner's goodies, the pewterer's wares, fans etc. . . . There is a cunning device for showing women's materials. Whether they are silks, chintzes, or muslins, they hang down in folds behind the fine, high windows so that the effect of this or that material, as it would be in the ordinary folds of a woman's dress, can be studied . . . First one passes a watch-making, then a silk or fan store, now a silversmith's, a china or glass shop. The spirit booths are particularly tempting . . . here flasks of every shape and form are exhibited: each one has a light behind which makes all the different coloured spirits sparkle. Just as alluring are the confectioners and fruiterers, where, behind the handsome glass windows pyramids of pink apples, figs, grapes, oranges and all manner of fruits are on show. We enquired the price of a pineapple and did not think it too dear at 6s. Most of all we admired the Argand lamps situated in a corner house and forming a really dazzling spectacle. Every variety of lamp, crystal, lacquer and metal ones, silver and brass in every possible shape.

Sophie in London 1786, being the diary of Sophie von La Roche, edited by Clare Williams, 1933, pp. 87, 141

5.14a Advertising

We think it of far more consequence to supply the People than the Nobility only; and though you speak contemptuously of Hawkers, Pedlars and those who supply Petty Shops, yet we must own that we think they will do more towards supporting a great Manufactory, than all the Lords in the Nation and however lofty your notions may be, We assure you we have no objection against pulling off our Hats and thanking them 4 times a Year and must beg you will allow us to do it. It is certain that Buckles . . . will sell, and therefore let it be understood, once for all, that we mean to follow the fashion of all Countries and confine our Sales to this World alone and to such members of it as will pay their debts and do their Business peacably, rationally, genteely and without incessant squabbling.

We have Agents in most parts of Europe, as well as in most of the great Towns in England, and we have considered London and its environs as your province; provided you take pains to supply every safe and respectable Dealer in Buckles from St James's Street down to Wapping.

Letter from Matthew Boulton to his London agent Richard Chippendall, 9 August 1794, quoted in Hoh-cheung and Lorna H. Mui, *Shops and Shopkeeping in Eighteenth Century England*, 1989, p. 18

5.14b   Richard Twining

The Sale of teas being now over, we take the liberty of troubling you with a list
of our prices . . .
    Our teas in general are remarkably fresh and good and we cannot omit this
opportunity of assuring our customers, that, in return for the many favours which
they have conferred upon us . . . they may depend upon every possible attention
on our part to supply them with the best teas at the most reasonable prices.
Your most obliged Humble Servant

Circular, 9 April 1785, quoted in *ibid.*, p. 266

5.14c   Advertising sugar

Unfortunately we have just received information of the loss of Grenada . . . which
has caused an advance in Raw sugar . . . Refined sugars are very scarce and dear,
but will be more Plenty in a Month or six Weeks, and hope cheaper . . . We shall
be glad to see you in Town if it suits your convenience, but if otherwise, shall
endeavour to execute any Orders you may favour us with, on the same terms and
with equal Attention.

**Circular from the London firm of Smith, Nash, Kemble and Travers,
wholesale-retail grocers, 1779, quoted in *ibid.*, p. 15**

5.14d   Selling razors

Rejoice! Rejoice! O ye mortals, at the good news of Packwood's new-invented
superior Razor Strop! By its power it will remove notches, if required, from any
small instrument; by its power it will give a most delectable smooth edge to a
razor, inasmuch that before the strop is proved, this advertisement is treated with
difference; but, after the trial, then what is the encomium? Why, that they are
worth their weight in gold, that the Proprietor deserves our thanks for so much
comfort we receive from his ingenuity, and we are lost in admiration!

Advertisement in *Oracle*, 11 June 1795

5.14e

The epithet of a WHET is quite the rage: a most curious genius has so successfully
WHETTED the inclinations of the people, that happy is the man now that can get a
WHET at Packwood's new invention.

***Norwich Mercury*, 11 July 1795**

5.14f

Seeing is believing, but feeling is the naked truth – Prejudiced as the public may be against the nostrums set forth in a flow of advertisements, merely to take the advantage of honest John Bull – yet there are some few exceptions allowed, and the merit due to PACKWOOD's superior Razor Strop is a proof to claim this exception; – the encomiums generally paid the proprietor are a little out of the common way, by those who have made trial of them . . .

Dublin Evening Post, 21 May 1796

5.15a Puffing attacked

The newspaper press is the greatest lying and puffing machine in the world! Then comes the walls with their barefaced falsehoods and the shop windows with their gilded lies.

James Dawson Burn, *The Language of the Walls and the Voice from the Shop Window or the Mirror of Commercial Roguery*, 1855, quoted in N. McKendrick *et al.*, *The Birth of a Consumer Society*, 1983, p. 148

5.15b

Puffing . . . seemed always to be carried on at the expense of the poor. There was the puffery of plate-glass and gas-light . . . and was it not evident that all this glitter and blaze must either increase the price of the articles sold or decrease the wages of those producing them?

Report of a speech by Henry Mayhew, *Morning Herald*, 29 October 1850

Questions

1 What methods for encouraging consumer spending can be found in documents **5.13** and **5.14a–f**?
2 At what social groups were they aimed? Justify your answer.
3 What was the basis of Matthew Boulton's argument in **5.14a**? How far do you think he had the correct business strategy?
4 There are important differences of language between documents **5.14b–c** and **5.14d–f**. What are they and why do you think they occurred?
5 In what ways was the approach to advertising in the eighteenth century 'modern' in character?
6 What was the basis for the attacks on puffing contained in documents **5.15a–b**? How far was the attack a moral one?

7 'Eighteenth- and early nineteenth-century advertising provide graphic
  evidence of the vitality of Britain's internal trade.' Discuss this
  statement.

The eighteenth and early nineteenth centuries saw an extension of Britain's
markets both internally and externally. Growing consumer demand, rising
population and improved transport facilities all contributed to growing trade.

6 Economic change: social and institutional bases

In many respects British society in the eighteenth and early nineteenth centuries was profoundly conservative. It is important for historians to explain how a society with such views and a traditional institutional structure could have generated change in so many areas of economic life. The context within which economic developments took place can enable historians to understand *why* they occurred. This chapter examines three areas which contributed to economic changes and considers the extent of each contribution.

A social context

Harold Perkin argued over twenty years ago that 'No one today would deny that the Industrial Revolution, that "vast increase of natural resources, labour, capital and enterprise" which began in Britain in the late eighteenth century . . . was a social revolution, at least in its effects' and that 'It [English society] syphoned off in every generation the newly rich and talented of the middle ranks, who might otherwise have been socially frustrated and politically discontented. France, where social climbing was frustrated, had a political revolution. Britain, where it was not, had an industrial one.'

Perkin pointed to the fluidity, the 'openness' and the lack of legal constraints in British society as central to understanding the economic developments that occurred. He saw the aristocracy as 'open' (though more recent writers like John Cannon and the Stones have called this into question) and unlike their continental counterparts who lived off custumal dues and labour services. The landed economy of the aristocracy was serviced, not by a repressed peasantry, but by landless wage labourers. Between these two social extremes lay a carefully graduated hierarchy, layer upon layer of occupational groups. It was an unequal society in which people were conscious of their status and position within this hierarchy, a situation reinforced by the mutually supportive ideologies of paternalism and deference. But English society, more than those of Wales, Scotland and Ireland, was remarkably capitalist in character and organisation, where the 'market' played a central role and 'enterprise' was recognised and, on occasions, rewarded. Defoe wrote in the early eighteenth century that:

> Wealth however got in England makes
> Lords of mechanics, gentlemen of rakes

and David Cannadine has suggested recently that 'The ultimate proof of success in business was the ability to leave it.'

6.1   Tawney on capitalism

The rational order of the universe is the work of God, and its plan requires that the individual should labour for God's glory. There is a spiritual calling and a temporal calling. It is the first duty of the Christian to know and believe in God; it is by faith that he will be saved. But faith is not a mere profession . . . The only genuine faith is the faith which produces works . . . The second duty of the Christian is to labour in the affairs of practical life, and this second duty is subordinate only to the first . . . From this reiterated insistence on secular obligations as imposed by the divine will, it follows that, not withdrawal from the world, but the conscientious discharge of the duties of business, is among the loftiest of religious and moral virtues . . . The idea of economic progress as an end to be consciously sought, while ever receding, had been unfamiliar to most earlier generations of Englishmen, in which the theme of moralists had been the danger of unbridled cupidity, and the main aim of public policy had been the stability of traditional relationships. It found a new sanction in the identification of labour and enterprise with the service of God . . . The worship of production and ever greater production – the slavish drudgery of the millionaire and his unhappy servants – was to be hallowed by the precepts of the same compelling creed.

R.H. Tawney, *Religion and the Rise of Capitalism*, 1926, Pelican edition, 1938, pp. 239, 247

6.2   Stewardship of wealth: a religious imperative

A good tradesman should never desire to be rich, a wise one never will be, but should do all he can with his own capital, to get all the money he can, and then to use it in the best way. A part must be devoted to religious purposes. How much? It must be decided by his own judgement. The whole of the rest should be used for charitable and useful purposes.

David Whitehead of Rawtenstall, *Autobiography*, typescript in Manchester Central Library, *c.* 1830, p. 81

6.3   William Fishwick of Burnley

The increase of his riches seemed rather to oppress him with the sense of increased responsibility, than to elate him with the notion of augmented influence, or the empty anticipation of luxurious delight. He sought by abounding liberality to guard against the otherwise inevitable dangers of prosperity.

W. Jessop, *An Account of Methodism in Rossendale*, Manchester, 1880, p. 248

Questions

1   How does R.H. Tawney explain the relationship between religion and business capitalism? How convincing do you find his argument?
2   In what ways do documents **6.2** and **6.3** provide support for the central role of religious belief in business success?
3   'Nonconformity seems to have been a crucial experience for several first-generation entrepreneurs, encouraging a set of values outwardly favourable to economic success.' Discuss this statement with reference to: (i) the emerging cotton industry; (ii) iron making; and (iii) woollen production.
4   Religious affiliation may have been a necessary prerequisite for entrepreneurial success but is it sufficient explanation? Explain your answer with reference to specific examples.

If the emergence of industrial capitalism cannot be fully explained by the thrusting morality of Nonconformity then it is important to examine other explanations for economic development. Entrepreneurial skills and 'enterprise' have long been recognised as essential for the creation of wealth and economic success. Three main explanations for the role of entrepreneurs seem possible. The first places entrepreneurs in their social environment and explains their emerging role either as the result of changes in the level of tolerance accorded to deviance from traditional norms of entrepreneurial activity or from changing attitudes to work in the broad social context. The second recognises the central role of entrepreneurship but maintains that it must be seen in relation to the conditioning of the workforce into the discipline of modern industrial organisation with its high degree of division of labour. The third explanation considers the capacity of a society to increase the number of energetic and innovative entrepreneurs and inventors in its total population. These explanations are not mutually exclusive. Historians who emphasise the role of religious belief in entrepreneurship tend to focus on business success as an expression of faith. By contrast, those who consider the importance of education tend to be concerned with the creation of a disciplined workforce as a prerequisite for entrepreneurial success.

6.4   Peter Gaskell

The men who did establish themselves were raised by their own efforts – commencing in a very humble way, and pushing their advance by a series of unceasing exertions, having a very limited capital to begin with, or even none at all save that of their own labour . . . the celerity with which some of these individuals accumulated wealth in the early times of steam spinning and weaving are proof – if any such were wanting – that they were men of quick views, great energy of character, and possessing no small share of sagacity; and were by these means able to avail themselves to the utmost of the golden advantages, which were presented to their grasp, from 1790 to 1817, a time when they supplied the whole universe with the products of manufacture . . . [These] men . . . had a practical acquaintance with machinery, and . . . laboured themselves, assiduously and diligently, [showing] that rapidity of action and quickness of calculation, which were essentially necessary to keep pace with the daily improvements projected and carried out around them.

P. Gaskell, *The Manufacturing Population of England*, London, 1833, pp. 45, 53–4

6.5   A more hostile view

First, then, as to the employers: with very few exceptions, they are a set of men who have sprung from the cotton-shop without education or address, except so much as they have acquired by their intercourse with the little world of merchants at the exchange at Manchester. They bring up their families at the most costly schools, determined to give their offspring a double portion of what they were so deficient in themselves.

'A Journeyman Cotton Spinner' in 1818, quoted in E.P. Thompson, *The Making of the English Working Class*, 1963, p. 199

6.6a   Education

I look upon it to be a good deal owing to the faults of Education – children are too often taught to construe a Latin book & write a good hand without ever being acquainted with the most useful truths of Natural philosophy which are far better suited to their capacities and far more agreeable to their inclinations than droning for years over a Latin Accidence which is often the case – the knowledge of things is much disregarded while that of words is too much attended to and which is the most useful as well as agreeable way every one will readily determine.

William Reynolds deploring the lack of interest in physics in 1777, quoted in A. Raistrick, *Dynasty of Ironfounders: The Darbys and Coalbrookdale*, 1953, p. 93

6.6b   View of Dr Erasmus Darwin

[He] thought it a very idle waste of time for any boys intended for trade to learn Latin, as they seldom learn it to any tolerable degree of perfection or retained what they learnt. Besides they did not want it, and the time would be much better bestowed in making themselves perfect in French and accounts . . .

Josiah Wedgwood to his partner Richard Bentley in 1779, quoted in S. Pollard, *The Genesis of Modern Management*, 1965, p. 132

6.6c   Education criticised

A youth designed for . . . any Mercantile Branch, has no occasion for spending his time at the University, or for a critical knowledge of the Dead Languages . . . At present, private Boarding Schools, called Academies, are preferred to the Public Seminaries, and, perhaps not without a deal of reason . . . [Seven years of] cramming a Boy's Head full of a Dead Language, of useless words, and incoherent terms, satiates his memory and confounds his judgment.

R. Campbell, *The London Tradesmen*, 1747, pp. 84–7

6.7   Entrepreneurs in the stocking industry

Mr Strutt had the satisfaction which was denied to his great prototype, Mr Lee, of realising a handsome fortune by his ingenuity in the hosiery and spinning manufactures, in conjunction with Sir Richard Arkwright, to whom he was a patron and partner. Few men had more real merit than Jedediah Strutt, as he possessed the singular qualities of being a good mechanic, a clever tradesman, and a patron of ingenuity in others . . .

This gentlemen [Thomas Maltby], though descended from and nearly related to a very respectable family at Hoveringham, near Southwell, had wrought in the frame as a journeyman for a considerable period. Being a person of some sagacity in manufacturing concerns, he represented the advantages of the new manufacture to his relatives so forcibly, that they agreed to advance him a competent sum of money to enable him to pursue the manufacture of lace, on a respectable scale . . .

This person was the venerable, the persevering, and indefatigable Mr William

Horton of Newgate-street, London, who, during a life protracted beyond the usual age allotted to man, has been sedulously employed in making various modifications upon the stocking frame . . . The finances of Horton, at the period in which he projected this invention, were very limited, and an unlucky accident was near depriving him of all means, at that juncture, of carrying his intention into effect . . . Fortunately he found a friend, who advanced him a few pounds, which enabled him to again complete his frame, upon finishing of which, having a small supply of money, he commenced his attempt to form a machine, for making knotted work from the stocking frame.

Gravenor Henson, *History of the Framework Knitters*, 1831, pp. 276, 313, 332–3

6.8   The second Robert Peel (1750–1830)

He was a favourable specimen of a class of men, who, availing themselves in Lancashire of the discoveries of other heads and of their own, and profiting by the peculiar local facilities for making and printing cotton goods as well as the wants and demands . . . for the articles manufactured, succeeded in realising great opulence, without possessing either refinement of manners, culture of intellect or more than commonplace knowledge.

W.A. Abrams, *Parish of Blackburn, County of Lancashire: A History of Blackburn, Town and Parish*, Blackburn, 1877, pp. 271–2

6.9   Setting up a firm

[In 1817] my brothers and I agreed that the firm should be called Thomas Whitehead and Brothers . . . Brother Peter attended to his warping and at nights assisted me in planning. He was very diligent and persevering. We had not been brought up mechanics but had good ideas of mechanism and we soon made a great improvement in our machinery . . . We had got a large stock of weft on hand which did not sell well. I bought some warps and began to manufacture. I got a few weavers in the neighbourhood of Balladenbrook. I got my mother who lived at New church to weave for us, and a few weavers more at New church . . . Balladenbrook was a small place and had no shop to sell food. The workpeople complained of having so far to go to buy other grocery . . . Warbourton, who had the mill of whom we took the room, had a woollen engine and carded woollen for country people. His business was not doing well for him. He said if we had no objections he would deliver the mill up to us. We went with him to Mr Hargreaves of whom he rented the mill, but did not agree with Mr Hargreaves about the mill at this time. We found that with all the money we could collect together we had little enough. We got mother to go and see if she could prevail of old Mr Thomas Hoyle of Manchester (Printer) to lend us a hundred pounds. My grandfather Lionel Blakey was one of the 'Friends' (called Quakers), as was also Thomas Hoyle. They were relations and fellow playboys . . .

David Whitehead of Rawtenstall, *Autobiography*, c. 1830, quoted in D. Lane, *The Industrial Revolution: The Birth of the Modern Age*, 1978, pp. 121–2

Questions

1 Compare the views expressed in documents **6.4** and **6.5**. Account for the differences in emphasis.
2 What education did contemporaries believe was necessary for success in business? Use documents **6.6a–c** to justify your answer.
3 In what respects does Gravenor Henson [**6.7**] provide an explanation for entrepreneurial success?
4 W.A. Abrams wrote his study of Blackburn in the 1850s. How far do you think this influenced his view of Peel and in what ways?
5 Autobiographies tend to justify an individual's existence. How does the autobiography of David Whitehead of Rawtenstall support this?
6 Using documents **6.1–6.9** produce a list of the characteristics of entrepreneurs in order of their importance. Justify your grading.
7 What impact have 'Victorian values' had on the ways recent historians have viewed entrepreneurship between 1750 and 1850?
8 'Without entrepreneurs there could have been no industrial revolution.' Discuss.

In his book *The Cotton Masters 1830–1860* Anthony Howe provides a comprehensive picture of the cotton masters of Lancashire through their social and political activities. This industrial elite played a leading role both within the British economy and within Lancashire itself. They were 'the pacemakers of economic change, a distinctive breed of newly wealthy men'. Tables **6.10a–e** raise the following important questions about the textile elite after 1830. How far were they 'self-made men' in the tradition of Samuel Smiles? What were their social origins? Where were they educated and what was their religious affiliation?

6.10a   **Table showing the masters: method of entry**

Sector	Hereditary	First generation
Cotton: pre-1800	6	13
1800–19	23	25
1820–29	46	42
1830–39	35	17
1840–49	42	24
No date	2	6
Calico-printing	11	25
Bleaching	13	3
Woollens, worsted	7	4
Silk	1	3
Flax	2	1
TOTAL	188	163

From A. Howe, *The Cotton Masters 1830–1860*, Oxford, 1984, p. 8

6.10b   **Table showing geographical origins of the masters**

Birthplace	Number	Percentage of total
Lancashire	265	80.3
Adjacent counties	26	7.9
Other northern counties	5	1.5
Midland counties	10	3.0
London, the south and west	6	1.8
Scotland	10	3.0
Ireland	3	0.9
Europe	5	1.5
ALL	330	99.9
Not traceable	21	

Ibid., p. 51

6.10c   Table showing socio-occupational origins of masters

| | Social class | | |
| | I | II | III |
Occupation of father			
1 Agriculture	—	18	—
2 Building	—	2	2
3 Dealing	15	3	7
4 Non-textile manufacture	4	1	2
5 Textiles	193*	4	6
6 Industrial service	2	—	—
7 Professional	7	1	—
8 Domestic service	—	2	—
9 Property owning/independent	9	1	—
TOTALS	230	30	19

Not known: 72

Key

Sample occupations:

Social class I: merchant, paper manufacturer (employing over 25 men), banker, clergyman, army officer, rentier

Social class II: yeoman, farmer, land surveyor, mining engineer, wholesale dealer, court draper, manager, journalist, quarry owner

Social class III: publican, plumber, mason, operative, butcher, barber

* The discrepancy with **6.10a** is accounted for by five men who established new firms rather than joining family ones.

Note: The classification of occupations and social classes is adapted from W.A. Armstrong, 'The use of information about occupation', in *Nineteenth Century Society*, (ed.) E.A. Wrigley, Cambridge, 1972, pp. 191–310

Ibid., p. 54

6.10d   Table showing education: highest level attained

	Hereditary	*First generation*	*Total*
Village, Dame Schools	—	5	5
Grammar schools	11	10	21
Private schools	15	5	20
Dissenting Academies	13	4	17
Public schools	14	3	17
Universities	13	3	16
Education abroad	5	—	5
Vocational education	4	1	5
TOTALS	75	31	106

Ibid., p. 55

6.10e   Table showing religious affiliation*

	Numbers of masters	*Percentage of those whose affiliation is known*
1 Church of England	145	49.7
2 Wesleyan Methodist	27 ⎫	10.6
3 Bible Christians	4 ⎭	
4 Presbyterians	7 ⎫	
5 Independent, Congregationalist	27 ⎬	12.3
6 Baptist	2 ⎭	
7 Unitarian	53	18.2
8 Quaker	15	5.1
9 Nonconformist unspecified	6	2.1
10 Swedenborgian	2 ⎫	
11 Moravian	1 ⎪	
12 Lutheran	1 ⎬	2.1
13 Roman Catholic	1 ⎪	
14 Jewish	1 ⎭	
TOTALS	292	100.1

Not known: 59

* Adult allegiance, thus excluding cases where only the religion of baptism is known.

Ibid., p. 62

Questions

1 **6.10a** shows the dates when firms were established and whether sons succeeded to a firm owned by their fathers or close relatives (hereditary) or whether they were new partnerships. What does it tell you about: (i) the development of the cotton industry; (ii) the nature of entrepreneurship; and (iii) the dominance of the cotton industry in Lancashire?

2 Only one woman is included in **6.10a**: Mary Bealey, of Mary Bealey & Sons, bleachers, Radcliffe. Why was business in Lancashire, as elsewhere, dominated by men?

3 What information about the geographical origin of the industrial elite can be found in **6.10b**?

4 What were the socio-occupational origins of the Lancashire industrial elite? In what ways does **6.10c** support or confound the Smilesian notion of the 'self-made man'?

5 Compare the educational standards of the industrial elite found in **6.10d**. Why do you think the second generation of textile masters were, on the whole, better educated than the first generation?

6 Explain the distribution of religious allegiances contained in **6.10e**. In what respects does it contradict the views of R.H. Tawney [**6.1**] and why?

7 'By the period 1830–60, the role of Dissent in innovation is not a crucial one; nevertheless, the religious affiliation of the "imitators" may reveal a particular distribution of Protestant virtues favourable to economic success, while it is resonant with implications for social and political attitudes' (*ibid.*, p. 61). Why did Dissent play such a major role in entrepreneurship?

8 Does the experience of Lancashire between 1830 and 1860 represent a loss of entrepreneurial zeal? Justify your answer.

Banking and credit

The eighteenth century saw an increase in the institutionalising of capital accumulation and investment. The most important of the new institutions that opened channels for the flow of capital were the banks. In England three main types of bank can be identified by 1750: the Bank of England which, though not yet a central bank with control over the money supply, had formalised its relationship with the Treasury since being founded in 1694; the London-based private banks and the country banks. Between them they provided accessibility to money, the easy circulation of which is of central importance to economic development.

6.11   Table showing money stock in circulation and means of payment (£m)

	1688	*1750*	*1775*	*1800*	*1811*	*1821*	*1831*	*1844*
Specie	10	15	16	20	15	18	30	36
Bank notes	2	5	10	25	45	32	29	28.5
Deposits	—	—	—	5	15	25	40	80.5
Total money [M1]	12	20	26	50	75	75	99	145
Other	8	20	37	115	140	76	67	75
Means of payment [M2]	20	40	63	165	215	151	166	220

From R.E. Cameron (ed.), **Banking in the Early Stages of Industrialisation**, Oxford, 1967, p. 42

Questions

1 In what ways did the total money (M1) change between 1688 and 1844 and why?
2 Why was there a decline in the amount of specie and increase in bank notes in circulation between 1800 and 1821?
3 Why was control over the money supply important in this period and how was this control effected?
4 'Banks were important for short-term loans but most fixed capital for investment was created by ploughing back profits into enterprises or borrowing from relatives and friends.' Discuss this statement.

The next set of documents relates to Ireland and is concerned with the issue of undercapitalisation in its economy. What role did banking services have in the Irish economy in the first half of the nineteenth century?

6.12a   A comparison

England has capital, Ireland has not; therefore England is rich and industrious, and Ireland is poor and idle. But where was the capital when England began to grow rich? It was the industry that made the capital, not the capital the industry . . . when money is made in England it is re-invested in the same or in a similar branch . . . until the amount of capital attains the vast dimensions which we now see.

Robert Kane, *The Industrial Resources of Ireland*, Dublin, 1845, p. 408

6.12b Investment in rent

The tenant willingly expends any capital he may possess in obtaining possession of the land and thus leaves himself without the means of tilling it effectively.

J.P. Kennedy, *Digest of Evidence Taken Before Her Majesty's Commissioners of Inquiry into the State of the Law and Practice in Respect to the Occupation of Land in Ireland* (Devon Commission), Dublin, 1847, p. 194

6.12c Need for drainage

It has been stated almost universally throughout the evidence, that the lands in nearly every district of Ireland require drainage; that the drainage and deep moving or subsoiling have proved most remunerative operations wherever they have been applied; that these operations have so far been introduced but to a very limited extent . . . it is impossible to imagine any other legitimate investment that could be expected to make so large a return.

***Ibid.*, pp. 14–15, 85**

6.12d Landlord attitudes

In Ireland we have to cultivate not the soil alone, but the peasant; and that ascending still higher in to social scale we have also to reform the character of the landlord. The latter will not prove light labour. He has to be taught and untaught much of what he has hitherto learned and acted on . . . too many of them betray palpable ignorance of the relations by which they stand connected with the rest of the community . . . This evil is sensibly aggravated by the number of those who, though possessed of only small estates of land will make no effort to better their condition . . . nine out of ten . . . will look upon themselves as independent country gentlemen and disdain the pursuits of commerce . . . such men are not saved from insolvency or ruin.

George Lewis Smyth, *Ireland, Historical and Statistical*, London, 1844–9, vol. III, pp. 81–3

6.12e   Seasonal nature of credit

Our business is almost entirely on one season of the year from the time of the harvest to the month of May. The principal business that we have for which money is required is business in butter, provisions and flax, which began to come to market then and such articles are almost always sold for cash, and the spinners require we lay in a stock of materials to last them for the whole year, and we frequently make advances to those people to be repaid to us in the summer, when their stock begins to diminish.

J.W. Bristow of the Northern Belfast Bank, *Secret Committee of the House of Lords on Commercial Distress,* **British Parliamentary Papers, 1847–8, vol. VIII, Q. 7340**

6.12f   Account holders at Ulster Bank branch in Aughnacloy, *c.* 1852

Attorney/solicitor	4	Linen manufacturer	1
Auctioneer	1	Mechanic	1
Baker	3	MD	2
Brewer/distiller	1	Millwright	1
Bridewell keeper	1	Policeman	2
Builder	1	Postmaster	1
'Butcher, postmaster and leather dealer'	1	'Private gentleman'	11
		Retired captain	1
Butter dealer	6	Road contractor	1
Carrier	1	Saddler	1
Clergyman	11	Shopkeeper	2
Cornmiller	2	Spade manufacturer	2
Draper	1	Spirit dealer	2
Farmer	121	Traveller	1
Flax dealer	1	Woollen draper	5
Grocer	16		
Haberdasher	4	Not in business	4
Innkeeper/publican	7	Unknown	12
Land agent	3	Total	239
Leather seller	1		
'Lieutenant'	1		

The village had a population of less than 2,000 in the 1851 Census, only one bank office and 'it may be presumed that the Ulster Bank . . . catered for a substantial proportion of the bank-using population in the village and surrounding area'.

Ulster Bank Aughnacloy Branch Records, printed in P. Ollerenshaw, *Banking in Nineteenth-century Ireland,* **Manchester, 1987, p. 82**

Questions

1 How far was the problem of undercapitalisation in the Irish agrarian economy one of social attitudes and why?
2 'It was not lack of capital but lack of confidence which accounted for the malaise in Ireland's economy between 1800 and 1850.' Discuss this statement.
3 In what respects do documents **6.12a–d** reflect an 'English' perspective of Ireland's problems?
4 How do documents **6.12e–f** cast doubt on the view of an Irish economy in crisis in the 1840s and 1850s?
5 What information about the social composition of bank depositors in agrarian Ireland can be obtained from **6.12f**?
6 'Ireland's economy had been significantly weakened by 1850 as a result of the dynamism of the economy in England.' Do you agree and why?

6.13a   Investment in bank shares by the 'poorer classes'

A great many of the poorer classes who had money in the savings bank were induced to become subscribers from the success which attended the management of the Northern Bank and the Provincial Bank [both in Belfast]; for instance there was a coach porter who took 150 guineas out of the savings bank and invested in the stock; a street constable, who had been 30 years engaged in making £300, which he invested likewise; many young men in offices, linen lappers, widow ladies and females seeking better interest on the faith of the respectability of the gentlemen who were appointed directors.

George Dundas, Belfast branch manager of the Agricultural and Commercial Bank in Belfast in *Select Committee on Joint Stock Banks*, British Parliamentary Papers, 1837, vol. XIV, QQ. 4143–7

6.13b   The Agricultural and Commercial Bank fails in 1840

The effect of small shares is to produce a numerous and ignorant body of shareholders, who will elect as directors the nominees of the men who made themselves most active in getting up the company without any regard whatever to their fitness for office. The natural effect will be fraud, neglect, confusion and ruin, while an appeal to the shareholders themselves will only make the confusion worse.

Mountifort Longfield, 'Banking and currency', *Dublin University Magazine*, vol. XVI, 1841, p. 380

Questions

1 What evidence is provided in **6.13a** about the attitudes of inhabitants of Belfast to savings and investment?

2 In what ways does this support the Smilesian notion of 'thrift'?

3 What are the major criticisms of the strategy of persuading the 'poorer classes' to invest in bank shares? Given that the Agricultural had failed how valid do you think these criticisms were? Or were they simply lessons learned in hindsight?

6.14a   The impact of the Famine

Deposits were withdrawn partly for the purpose of lending that money on higher rates to some railways; and with us there have been for some time local improvements which we have been carrying on in the harbour and town, and pipe water, and part of our deposits was taken out and lent upon the security of those works, but still a good many small deposits have been drawn out from the necessities of people obliging them to have their money.

Secret Committee of the House of Lords on Commercial Distress, British Parliamentary Papers, 1847–8, vol. VIII, Q. 7220

6.14b   Table showing deposits in Irish joint-stock banks 1840–51 (£)

Year	Amount	Increase	Decrease
1840	5,567,851	—	—
1841	6,022,573	454,722	—
1842	6,416,795	394,222	—
1843	6,965,681	548,886	—
1844	7,601,421	635,740	—
1845	8,031,044	429,623	—
1846	8,493,133	411,089	—
1847	6,493,124	—	1,949,009
1848	7,071,122	577,998	—
1849	7,469,675	398,553	—
1850	8,268,838	799,163	—
1851	8,263,091	—	5,747

All figures at 31 December.

From W. Neilson Hancock, *Report on Deposits in Joint-Stock Banks in Ireland 1840–65*, Dublin, 1866

Questions

1 What evidence is provided by these two documents of the impact of the Famine?
2 'Awareness of diversification opportunities in Ireland during the 1840s depended on whether people lived in the north and east or the south and west of the country.' Discuss this statement with reference to the impact of the Famine on investment and savings in Ireland.
3 'There was no real financial crisis in Ireland in the 1840s.' 'The real crisis in Ireland was social rather than economic.' Compare the validity of these two statements.

The role of government

The role of government in the mid eighteenth century differed from the usual function of governments in countries undergoing economic development today where they act as producers, entrepreneurs and providers of capital in order to promote high rates of economic growth. In 1750 the task of successive governments was to regulate a private enterprise economy organised around the market. State action was much less conspicuous and examples of direct intervention are few. There were no state factories, as for example in France, no state scientific institutes as in Prussia and no state economic plans. The role of government was to support and facilitate the development of what has been called 'the wealth instinct'. Its function was indirect rather than directive, creating the institutional framework within which economic changes could occur. For contemporaries the debate on the role of government hinged on certain questions: how far should government guide the economy in certain, predetermined directions? what degree of regulation was both necessary and acceptable? how far could regulation frustrate individual enterprise? should protection be afforded to key sectors of the economy? in what ways should labour be protected against exploitation? Sir Dudley North identified the issue succinctly in his *Discourse on Trade* in 1691: 'We may labour to hedge in the Cuckoo, but in vain; for no People ever yet grew rich by Policies, but it is Peace, Industry and Freedom that brings Trade and Wealth, and nothing else.' J.R. McCulloch wrote in an editorial in *The Scotsman* in August 1823 that 'Liberal and not restrictive laws . . . were the source of England's prosperity.'

6.15   In retrospect

Railways have become an Empire within the Empire . . . the experience of forty years has brought conclusive proof of the grave initial mistake made in the relations between the State and the railways. It would have been well if large powers of State interference had been insisted upon from the very first. As this was not done, it remains only to create them now that the need for them has been amply demonstrated . . . State interference is not safely to be dispensed with in face of the gigantic forces which railway enterprise had called into being.

The Times, 1884, quoted in H. Parris, *Government and the Railways in Nineteenth Century Britain*, 1965, p. vii

6.16   David Ricardo criticises apprenticeship legislation

He thought it was a maxim, that no person ought to be controlled in his own arrangements, unless such control was rendered necessary by paramount political circumstances. Now, no such necessity could be shown in support of this bill [William Huskisson had sponsored legislation to require all operators of merchant ships to have a number of apprentices in proportion to tonnage] . . . He denied that this bill would cause an addition of one seaman to the number now in service. So long as there was employment for seamen, there would be encouragement enough for them; and when there was not, those who were now here, would resort to foreign countries for employ. The only effect of the bill would be, to reduce the wages of seamen; and that alone would render it objectionable.

Hansard, Second Series, vol. 8, 24 March 1823, p. 663

6.17   Howich supports factory legislation

While I subscribe to the principle in the sense in which it was meant to be laid down by the distinguished author I have quoted,* I utterly deny that it applies to the question now before us . . . I contend that you altogether misapply the maxim of leaving industry to itself when you use it as an argument against regulations of which the object is, not to increase the productive power of the country, or to take the fruits of a man's labour from himself and give it to another, but, on the contrary, to guard the labourer himself and the community from the evils against which the mere pursuit of wealth affords us no security. The welfare, both moral and physical of the great body of the people, I conceive to be the true concern of the Government: national wealth, no doubt, rightly used, greatly contributes to that welfare, but he must indeed have a low and mean idea of our nature, who thinks that mere wealth is all in all to a nation, and who does not see that in the too eager pursuit of wealth, a nation like an individual, may neglect what is of infinitely higher importance.

* Howich, an admirer of Adam Smith, had quoted the passage from Smith that begins 'The property which every man has in his own labour, as it is the original foundation of all other property, so it is the most sacred and inviolable.'

Hansard, Third Series, vol. 74, 3 May 1844, pp. 641–3

6.18 George Julius Poulett Scrope attacks the Corn Laws

The hon. Member does not seem to be aware that the principle he declaims against as a cold dogma of a stern political ecomomy is the one sole vivifying principle of all commerce – the stimulus to all improvement – the mainspring of civilization – the principle, namely, of obtaining the largest and best result at the least cost – in other words, to get the most you can of what you want for your money or your labour . . . I call on you then no longer to interfere between the people and their spontaneous supplies of food – no longer by unwise and unjust law to prevent the industrious classes of this country from availing themselves of the ample means which God and nature have placed at their disposal for obtaining, by the exercise of their unrivalled skill and energy, an abundant supply of the first necessaries of life.

Ibid., vol. 83, 20 February 1846, pp. 1279, 1283

6.19 Peel on financing Irish railways

If these railroads were likely to turn out profitable speculations, why not leave them to the spontaneous exertions of the landowners and capitalists of Ireland? If they were likely to turn out unprofitable speculations, let them consider the unfairness of what they were about to do.

Ibid., vol. 45, 1 March 1839, p. 1089,

6.20 Macaulay opposes legislative restriction

I believe that I am as firmly attached as any Gentleman in this House to the principle of free trade properly stated, and I should state that principle in these terms: that it is not desirable that the State should interfere with the contracts of persons of ripe age and sound mind, touching matters purely commercial. I am not aware of any exceptions to the principle; but you would fall into error if you apply it to transactions which are not purely commercial . . . the principle of non-interference is one that cannot be applied without great restriction where the public health or the public morality is concerned.

Ibid., 22 May 1846

Questions

1 What arguments are put forward in documents **6.16–6.20** in favour of and against state intervention in the economy?
2 What was 'the principle of free trade properly stated' [**6.20**]?

3 'The welfare, both moral and physical of the great body of the people, I conceive to be the true concern of the Government . . .' [6.17]. What did Howich mean by this? In what ways did it contradict the principles of free trade?

4 *The Times* in 1884 [6.15] suggested that state intervention in railways should have occurred. Why?

5 In what ways could the arguments enunciated in 6.15 be extended to other branches of the economy between 1750 and 1850?

6 'Britain was never a laissez-faire state.' Discuss this statement in relation to: (i) the economy; and (ii) social reforms in the first half of the nineteenth century.

7 'Between 1750 and 1850 the British state had a regulatory role over the economy, but that role was more often indirect than direct.' How far is this statement valid?

8 'The role of Political Economy in the development of both the British economy and the British state was frequently misunderstood by contemporaries and subsequently by historians.' How do you react to this statement and why?

Any examination of the social and institutional bases for economic change needs to distinguish between the intentional and unintentional consequences of actions and events. The social structure was adaptable and flexible but it could also be reactionary and traditional in attitude. Banking and credit provided investment opportunities for entrepreneurial activity, but institutionalising 'risk' could stifle enterprise. It is paradoxical that laissez-faire, spawned by Political Economy, should be seen by contemporaries and later historians as the epitome of an economic system which was, by its increasingly complex nature, to become far more regulated than its early eighteenth century precursor. There was no blueprint produced by the state for the economic changes that occurred, yet without the framework of social and institutional structures the extent and even the nature of change may well have been different. Ultimately it was individuals, on their own or with others, not rhetoric or theory who made change possible. Economic policies facilitated or retarded change, they did not create it.

Bibliography

General works

Ashton, T.S., *The Industrial Revolution 1760–1830*, Oxford University Press, 1948. A straightforward, if slightly dated, introduction

Berg, M., *The Age of Manufacture 1700–1820*, Fontana, 1985. Eminently readable

Brown, R., *Society and Economy in Modern Britain 1700–1850*, Routledge & Kegan Paul, 1991. This takes a 'British' perspective

Cannadine, D., *The Pleasures of the Past*, Collins Publishers, 1989. A stridently witty review

Clapham, J., *An Economic History of Modern Britain*, vol. 1: *The Early Railway Age 1820–1850*, Cambridge University Press, 1926. A 'classic' work which contains much of value

Crafts, N.F.R., *British Economic Growth during the Industrial Revolution*, Oxford University Press, 1985. This puts forward a revisionist perspective

Deane, P., *The First Industrial Revolution*, Cambridge University Press, 1983

Digby, A. and Feinstein, C. (eds.), *New Directions in Economic and Social History*, Macmillan, 1989. A useful collection of papers which summarises recent developments

Floud, R. and McCloskey, D. (eds.), *The Economic History of Britain since 1700*, vol. 1: *1700–1800*, Cambridge University Press, 1981. This provides a 'New Economic History' approach and should be read in conjunction with Cannadine (1989) above

Halevy, E., *A History of the English People in the Nineteenth Century*, vol. 1: *England in 1815*, new edition with introduction by A. Briggs, Ark, 1987. Another 'classic'

Mathias, P., *The First Industrial Nation*, Methuen, 2nd edition, 1983

Mathias, P. and Davis, J.A., *The First Industrial Revolution*, Basil Blackwell, 1989. Another collection of papers which summarises recent developments

May, T., *An Economic and Social History of Britain 1760–1970*, Longman, 1987

More, C., *The Industrial Age: Economy and Society 1750–1985*, Longman, 1989

Wrigley, E.A., *Continuity, Chance and Change: The Character of the Industrial Revolution in England*, Cambridge University Press, 1988. This also puts forward a revisionist perspective

Population

Malthus, T.R., *An Essay on the Principle of Population*, first published 1798, Penguin Books Ltd, 1970. Good for contemporary attitudes

Tranter, N., *Population and Society 1750–1940*, Longman, 1985. A good summary of existing knowledge

Winch, D., *Malthus*, Oxford University Press, 1987. Also good for contemporary attitudes

Wrigley, E.A. and Schofield, R.S., *The Population History of England 1541–1871: A Reconstitution*, Cambridge University Press, 1989. Difficult but fundamental

Agriculture

Beckett, J.V., *The Agricultural Revolution*, Basil Blackwell, 1990. A straightforward introduction

Brown, R., *Change and Continuity in British Society 1800–1850*, Cambridge University Press, 1987

Chambers, J.D. and Mingay, G.E., *The Agricultural Revolution 1750–1880*, Batsford, 1966

Mingay, G.E. (ed.), *The Victorian Countryside*, 2 vols., Routledge & Kegan Paul, 1980. An invaluable collection of essays, as is:

Mingay, G.E. (ed.), *The Agrarian History of England and Wales*, vol. 6: *1750–1850*, Cambridge University Press, 1989

Turner, M.E., *Enclosure in Britain 1750–1830*, Macmillan, 1984. A summary of the debate on enclosure

Industrial development

Bythell, D., *The Sweated Trades*, Batsford, 1978

Bythell, D., 'Cottage Industry and the Factory System', *History Today*, April 1983. An examination of the nature of industrial organisation and the persistence of the 'domestic' system

Chapman, S.D., *The Cotton Industry in the Industrial Revolution*, Macmillan, 2nd edition, 1987

Church, R. (ed.), *The Dynamics of Victorian Business*, Allen and Unwin, 1983. A general overview

Clarkson, L.A., *Proto-Industrialisation: The First Phase of Industrialisation*, Macmillan, 1985. A summary of the debate on the nature of industrial organisation

Flinn, M.W., *A History of the British Coal Industry*, vol. 2: *The Industrial Revolution 1700–1830*, Oxford University Press, 1984

Harris, J.R., *The British Iron Industry 1700–1850*, Macmillan, 1988

Musson, A.E., *The Growth of British Industry*, Batsford, 1978. Another general overview

Papers on water and wind power, *History Today*, March 1980

Thomis, M., *Responses to Industrialisation*, David and Charles, 1976. A more detailed examination of industrial organisation and the 'domestic' system

Von Tunzelmann, G.N., *Steam Power and British Industrialization to 1860*, Oxford University Press, 1978

Communications

Aldcroft, D.H. and Freeman, M.J. (eds.), *Transport and the Industrial Revolution*, Manchester, 1983. A useful collection of articles

Bagwell, P.S., *The Transport Revolution since 1770*, Batsford, 1974. A broad survey

Dyos, H.J. and Aldcroft, D.H., *British Transport*, Penguin Books Ltd, 1976. Another general survey

Gourvish, T.R., *Railways and the British Economy 1830–1914*, Macmillan, 1980. A summary of much research

Perkin, H., *The Age of the Railway*, Routledge, 1970. Another general overview

Entrepreneurship and business

Crouzet, F. (ed.), *Capital Formation and the Industrial Revolution*, Methuen, 1967. This contains useful articles

Crouzet, F., *The First Industrialists*, Cambridge University Press, 1986. An examination of the eighteenth-century entrepreneur which should be compared with Payne (1988) below

Hoppit, J., *Risk and Failure in English Business 1700–1800*, Cambridge University Press, 1987. This looks at the downside of business

Hudson, P., *The Genesis of Industrial Capital*, Cambridge University Press, 1986. An essential study

Payne, P.L., *British Entrepreneurship in the Nineteenth Century*, Macmillan, 2nd edition, 1988

Pollard, S., *The Genesis of Modern Management*, Penguin Books Ltd, 1968. This looks broadly at the emergence of modern forms of manufacturing

A British perspective

Cullen, L.M., *An Economic History of Ireland since 1660*, Batsford, 1972. This provides a radical interpretation, as does:

Cullen, L.M., *The Emergence of Modern Ireland 1600–1900*, Batsford, 1981

Foster, R.S., *Modern Ireland 1600–1972*, Allen Lane, 1988. This has much information on economic matters

Jenkins, G.H., *The Foundations of Modern Wales, 1642–1780*, Oxford University Press, 1987

Jones, G.E., *Modern Wales*, Cambridge University Press, 1984. A good general survey which should be supplemented by Jenkins (1987) above

Kearney, H., *The British Isles: A History of Four Nations*, Cambridge University Press, 1989. A novel and readable chronological study

Lyons, F.S.L., *Ireland since the Famine*, Fontana, 1973. This also has much on economic affairs

Smout, T.C., *A History of the Scottish People 1560–1830*, Collins Publishers, 1969. Essential

Smout, T.C., *A Century of the Scottish People 1830–1950*, Collins Publishers, 1986. Essential

Index